IN OUR OWN IMAGE

An African American History

The Peoples Publishing Group, Inc.
and the Rochester City School District

The Peoples Publishing Group, Inc.
Free to Learn, to Grow, to Change

Project Manager, *Doreen Smith*
Copy Editor, *Grant Hansen*
Cover Design, *Jeremy Mayes, Doreen Smith, Leon Wilburn*
Design, *Doreen Smith & Jeremy Mayes*
Illustrations, *Armando Baéz*
Maps, *Doreen Smith & Mapping Specialist*
Production/Electronic Design, *Doreen Smith, Kristine Liebman & Brooke Kaska*
Photo Research, *Kristine Liebman, Brooke Kaska*

The Peoples Publishing Group, Inc.

Free to Learn, to Grow, to Change

ISBN 1-56256-041-7

© 1998

The Peoples Publishing Group, Inc.
299 Market St.
Saddle Brook, NJ 07663

10 9 8 7 6 5

TABLE OF CONTENTS

TABLE OF CONTENTS

TABLE OF CONTENTS

TABLE OF CONTENTS

IN OUR OWN IMAGE

An African American History

**The Peoples Publishing Group, Inc.
and the Rochester City School District**

The Peoples Publishing Group, Inc.

Free to Learn, to Grow, to Change

AFRICAN ORIGINS

800-1492

◈ The ritual of dance was important in many ancient African cultures.

This symbol originated in Northern Nigeria and was created to look like a relief design on a mud wall.

When Americans trace their ancestors, they find the geographic area and the people from which they came. For example, Americans whose ancestors came from Italy are called Italian Americans. Americans whose ancestors came from Poland are called Polish Americans. In the same way, Americans whose ancestors came from Africa are called African Americans. Native Americans are the only people who believe that their ancestors came from this hemisphere.

In early American history, African Americans were often referred to by their color or as slaves. African Americans, however, referred to themselves by their country of origin. In the 1600s, people from West Africa might call themselves Yoruba or Ibo. These were two nations in West Africa. In the 1600s, people from either of these nations would never have used skin color to describe themselves.

The ancestors of African Americans came from many different nations, regions and cultures in Africa. When they came to America, they brought with them the ideas, experiences and skills that helped to build this country. African Americans are descendants of people from highly developed civilizations that are thousands of years old.

 This is a tenth-century bronze portrait head of a royal family member from the ancient Ife civilization.

Millions of African people were enslaved and forced to come to America to work for European Americans. However, the term "slavery" refers to the working and living conditions of these people. It is not correct to refer to the ancestors of African Americans only as slaves. The following chapters will explain that many of the earliest African people who came to America were not slaves. Also, very few Africans were slaves in their own countries before they were forced to come here.

To say that "African people came to America as slaves" is too general a statement. It describes African Americans in only one way. It is not true because it gives an incomplete picture.

Ask yourself this question: Is someone a "slave" or a "person" first? Was Frederick Douglass "the most famous slave who escaped to freedom," or was Frederick Douglass "a famous African American who once was enslaved, but escaped to freedom?" Do you see the difference? In the first statement, Frederick Douglass is described only as a famous slave. In the second example, Frederick Douglass is described as a famous African American, who was an enslaved person at one time. Frederick Douglass was not famous because he was enslaved. He was famous because of the many contributions he made to American life. To describe him only as a famous slave limits what you can know and feel about him. The exercises on pages 7 through 9 will help you to see that the way people are described can affect how you think and feel about them and about yourself.

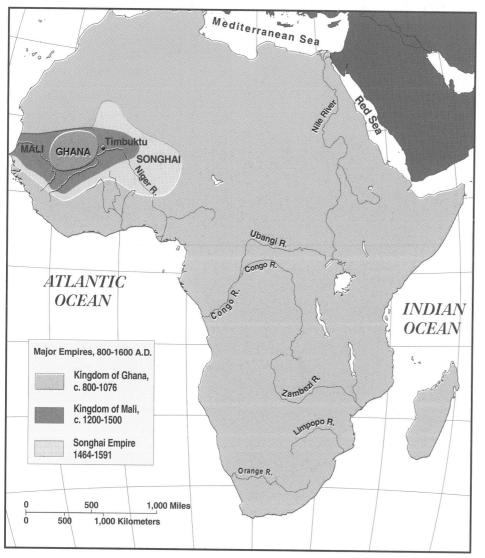

Major Empires, 800-1600 A.D.

Kingdom of Ghana, c. 800-1076

Kingdom of Mali, c. 1200-1500

Songhai Empire 1464-1591

```
0        500      1,000 Miles
0    500     1,000 Kilometers
```

The ancestors of many African Americans came from the west coast of Africa. There were three major empires in West Africa from 800-1600 A.D. Mali rose to power in 1200 after Ghana and the empire of Songhay was powerful from the 1400s to the 1600s. During this time, the great city of Timbuktu, shown on page 5, was a city of more than 100,000 people. It was a wealthy center of finance, learning and culture.

Our African Heritage

The map of Africa on page 4 shows the location of ancestral homes of many African Americans. There were three major empires in West Africa between 800-1600 A.D. Between 800-1000, Ghana was the most powerful country in West Africa. Mali rose to power in 1200 and the empire of Songhay was powerful from the 1400s to the 1600s. During this time, the great city of Timbuktu was a city of more than 100,000 people. It was a wealthy center of finance, learning and culture.

African history is hundreds of thousands of years old. Its people and cultures are responsible for the earliest developments of humanity and for the building of great civilizations in Ethiopia, Kemet, Merue, Nubia, Kanem, Ghana, Mali, Songhay and Congo. Greek scholars paid tribute in their writings to African culture and African scholars.

Long before Columbus came to the Americas in 1492, there were wealthy cities in Ghana, Mali and Songhay. In the 15th and 16th centuries, Timbuktu, a city of more than 100,000 people, was known as a center of finance, culture, and learning. Its University of Sankore taught law and surgery. It had a library with a large and valuable collection of books written in Greek, Latin and Arabic. Even before 600 A.D., and up through the 17th century, African cities and towns traded gold and goods with Indian, Chinese, Arab and European traders.

 The great city of Timbuktu during the Songhay Empire, 1400s to 1600s, was a center of learning and commerce.

Hundreds of years before Europe and America looked to Africa as a large source of free labor, many Africans traveled to Europe. Some stayed there to live. In fact, the ancestors of the first African Americans in Jamestown were West Africans who had been living in Europe for several generations.

In the 1500s, bright young African men of the ruling classes went to Lisbon and Rome to study. African and European kings exchanged letters and gifts. On May 15, 1518, Henry of the Congo, Africa, led a mission to the Vatican and formally addressed the Pope in Latin. In Rome, Lisbon and other European centers, Africans rose to high positions in the church and the state. At this time, race and color were not important factors. Europe and Africa saw that each had something to offer the other.

West African civilization began to decline in the 16th and 17th centuries. At the same time, the American colonists were looking for a vast source of free labor. Europe took advantage of this decline and used gun powder to dominate parts of Africa. African societies were further weakened by the kidnapping and enslaving of millions of their people.

African history is vast, complex and rich. Africa has made great contributions in the sciences, the arts, agriculture, crafts, architecture, music, religion and philosophy. There is much to learn and much yet to be discovered about our common heritage. One thing is certain—the millions of Africans who came to America and their descendants come from a long tradition that has greatly contributed and continues to contribute to the development of the United States of America.

King and Queen of the prosperous West African city of Benin, about 1400 A.D.

ACTIVITY

Two Views:
What Do They Tell You?

Read each set of sentences. On a separate sheet of paper, write the words or phrases that are different in each writing. How are the two passages different in what they say? Which is most correct? Why?

SET 1

A. Frederick Douglass was the most famous slave who escaped to freedom.

B. Frederick Douglass, a famous African American, was once enslaved. He escaped and gained his freedom in 1838.

SET 2

A. The owners of many big Southern plantations used slaves to work their land. These slaves were African people who had been kidnapped from their homeland. The kidnapped Africans were bought and sold as pieces of property. By 1750, there were about 250,000 slaves living and working on plantations in the South.

B. By 1750, there were about 250,000 African Americans who lived and worked as slaves on Southern plantations. At this same time, there were also African Americans who lived and worked as free men and women in the North and South.

SET 3

A. Most immigrants came to America because they wanted to. However, the ancestors of one group of Americans were forced to come to this country. About 200 years ago, many people were taken from their homes in Africa and brought to the Americas to be slaves. More than 100 years ago, slavery was outlawed in the United States, but peoples of African descent have had to fight long and hard to win their full rights as American citizens.

B. Most immigrants wanted to come to America. Most ancestors of one group of Americans, however, were forced to come. Hundreds of years ago, millions of free people from Africa were kidnapped from their homes and forced to come to the Americas to work as slaves. More than 100 years ago, slavery was outlawed in the United States but African Americans have had to fight long and hard to gain and to keep the full rights of American citizens.

As you continue to read, pay attention to how people are described. Notice how descriptions can affect how you think and feel about groups of people. Bring any other examples of this that you find to the attention of your class. Be a critical reader.

ACTIVITY

Choose A or B and follow the directions. Consider including your writing in your writing portfolio.

A. Using a separate sheet of paper, write a paragraph using the following as your first sentence.

Frederick Douglass was the most famous slave who escaped to freedom.

B. Using a separate sheet of paper, write a paragraph using the following statements as your opening.

Frederick Douglass, a famous African American, was once enslaved. He escaped and took his freedom in 1838.

FREDERICK DOUGLASS
from Youth to Old Age

1. Frederick Douglass was enslaved until he was 21 years old.

3. Frederick Douglass as a middle aged man continued to fight for what he believed.

2. Frederick Douglass as a young man beginning his work as an abolitionist

4. Frederick Douglass in his later years

Write your answers on a separate piece of paper.

VOCABULARY TO KNOW

Use context clues or a dictionary to help you write definitions for the following words:

1. ancestor
2. geographic
3. hemisphere
4. descendant

5. kidnapped
6. contribution
7. limits
8. civilization

Thinking Critically

1. Name two African nations of which many African Americans are descendants.

2. Explain how the earliest African people who came to America helped to build this country.

Writing

3. Explain the difference between the use of the word "slaves" in the following sentences:

   a. Africans were brought to America as slaves.

   b. Africans were forced to come to America to work as slaves.

4. Write a composition describing African people who were forced to come to America in the 1600s.

THE FIRST AFRICAN EXPLORERS AND SETTLERS IN AMERICA

1400-1650

 Early arrivals in Jamestown set out to make a new home for themselves in America.

This symbol originated in Kinshasha, Congo, and was created to decorate cloth.

3 1833 04662 6757

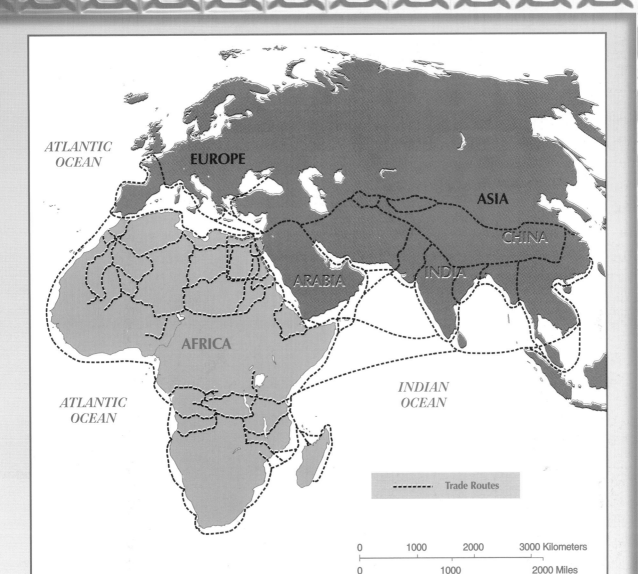

 African people traded with many places before 600 A.D.

ven before 600 A.D., African cities and towns were exchanging gold and goods with Chinese, Indian, Arab and European traders. Through this trade, Europe came to know about some of the large wealthy cities on the west coast of Africa. One of these cities, Timbuktu was located in the country of Mali in West Africa. More than 100,000 people lived in Timbuktu. In the 1400s and 1500s, Timbuktu was a great center of business and learning. The University of Sankore was there. It had a large library and taught law and medicine. Some scholars from Greece came to study there.

Look at a globe or a map of the world. Notice how close Africa is to Italy, Spain and Portugal. In the 1500s, bright young African men who were the sons of rulers went to Rome, the capital of Italy, and to Lisbon, the capital of Portugal, to study. Other Africans went to Europe for religious reasons. In 1518, Henry of the Congo, Africa, led a mission to Rome. He spoke to the Pope in Latin. Some of these early African visitors stayed in Europe. Some rose to high places in the churches and the governments of Rome, Lisbon and other European cities.

The Slave Trade Begins

The largest number of Africans came to Europe because of Prince Henry the Navigator of Portugal. He had heard about the wealth in Africa. In 1444, Portugese sailors were exploring the west coast of Africa. They kidnapped about 70 Africans and took them back to Portugal to Prince Henry. Within ten years, 1,000 Africans were taken by force each year. By the mid-1500s, Spain and Portugal had large numbers of Africans. Some of these men and women were made servants or slaves. Others had become free.

 Portugese sailors kidnapped Africans from the interior of Africa and forced them to leave their homes to board the slave ships that waited on the coast.

Descendants of the first Africans to live in Spain and Portugal accompanied Columbus on his trip to America.

Columbus. Nino was the pilot of one of Christopher Columbus's ships. Other African men traveled with Pizarro to Peru. In 1565, they helped to build the first city for settlers in the Americas. It was called St. Augustine (located in Florida today). African men were also with Cortez in Mexico. One of these men planted and harvested the first wheat crop in the Americas.

Estevanico was the first African American to enter Arizona and New Mexico as part of a European expedition.

African Explorers in America

In 1513, thirty African men were with Balboa when he reached the Pacific Ocean. The best known of the early African explorers was Estevanico, who

Spain and Portugal sent explorers to the Americas in the 1500s. African people traveled with the explorers. They were the descendants of the first Africans who lived in Spain and Portugal. Several African men, including Pedro Alonzo Nino, sailed with

explored Florida in 1528. A few years later, he led the first expedition for Spain to what is now New Mexico and Arizona.

Indentured African Servants

African men also came with French explorers to North America. They traveled down the Mississippi River with Marquette and Joliet. They served as farmers, blacksmiths, carpenters and masons in several French settlements. In 1765, Jean Baptiste Du Sable came to New France. He explored the area that is now Chicago. He built a trading post at the mouth of the Chicago River. He is known as the founder of Chicago.

 In the early 1600s, tobacco became the money crop in the Virginia colony. African and European indentured servants worked the fields together. When their terms of indenture were over (usually three to seven years), they became free.

African men and women came to the English settlements in a different way. They came as indentured servants—the same way that many of the first poor Europeans came. They sold themselves or were sold into a system of indenture that lasted from three to seven years. In Jamestown, Virginia, in 1619, twenty Africans were sold into indenture by a Dutch ship captain. He robbed a Spanish ship on its way to the West Indies and took the Africans who were on the ship. In 1621, immigrants aboard the **James**, a ship from England, arrived in the Virginia colony. One of the immigrants was an African man called Antonio. In 1623, John Pedro arrived from England. Pedro was also of African descent. For the next forty or more years, many African people came to many of the English colonies.

Early records in Virginia refer to early African settlers as servants, not as slaves. In 1649, colonial leaders reported that "there are in Virginia about fifteene [early spelling] thousand English and of Negroes brought thither, three hundred good servants."[1] By the 1650s, some African settlers owned land and had their own servants. In other colonies, such as Massachusetts, records up to the 1700s call African people "servants," not "slaves."

Most of these servants became free after their terms of indenture, or a work contract. They worked together

[1] *Before the Mayflower*, Lerone Bennett, 1982

IN OUR OWN IMAGE

and mixed with poor whites as equals. At that time in American history, poor whites and poor Africans were of the same social group, or class. Race and color were not important. What separated one group of people from another was being a servant or being free. In the mid-1600s, people of European and African descent were in both groups.

In the following chapters, you will learn why this situation changed in the colonies. You will learn how racism and prejudice came about in the colonies.

 Poor white Europeans also served terms of indenture. When their time of indenture was completed, both African and European people received the same opportunities.

ACTIVITY

JEAN BAPTISTE DU SABLE

1. What large American city did this man found?

2. On a separate sheet of paper, answer the above question by writing a story about this man.

Write your answers on a separate piece of paper.

VOCABULARY TO KNOW

Use context clues or a dictionary to help you write definitions for the following words:

1. mission
2. class
3. harvested
4. expedition
5. indenture
6. mason
7. immigrant
8. prejudice

Thinking Critically

1. What were some reasons Africans went to Europe in the 1400s and the 1500s? Why did some Europeans go to Africa during this period?

2. Name some of the expeditions to the New World that involved African men. Explain what each accomplished.

3. Explain how Africans came to the English colonies.

Writing

4. Write a short paragraph describing the ways that Africans and Europeans met in the 1400s and 1500s.

5. Pretend you are John Pedro in 1623 and have just arrived in Virginia on the *Swan*. You are going to be an indentured servant. Describe what you think that means and what you hope to do when your term of service is over.

THE EUROPEAN SLAVE TRADE

1620-1750

From 1619 to the 1660s, African people who came to the English colonies in America were indentured servants. In the picture above, twenty African men, women and children are being sold as indentured servants to landowners in Jamestown, Virginia, in 1619. An indentured servant was not a slave, but free after the time of servitude was finished.

This symbol originated in Benin, Nigeria, and was created to look like a carved wood pattern.

Much of the work in the early colonies was done by indentured servants. They were poor Europeans, Native Americans and Africans.

If Africans were not slaves at first, why did they become enslaved? Remember that twenty Africans came to Jamestown in 1619. The first Africans in Jamestown were indentured servants, not slaves. Sometime between 1609 and 1664, people with many different backgrounds walked the streets in New Amsterdam (what is now New York City). There were Native Americans, Europeans and people from African countries. Do you think Africans in New Amsterdam were indentured servants or slaves between 1609 and 1664? This is what is known from historical records:

> The Dutch settled Manhattan Island in 1609. At that time, no difference in status was made among Native Americans, Europeans and Africans.

> In 1664, the Dutch went to war with the English and lost. As a result, New Netherlands became New York. New Amsterdam became New York City.

In 1664, New York passed a law that changed the status of Africans. The Africans became slaves.

Africans had not been slaves in New Amsterdam. They were

ANTHONY JOHNSON

Anthony Johnson came to the Virginia colony as an indentured servant. He came from England in 1621 and finished his term of indenture within a few years. He began to buy property. In 1651, he paid for five indentured servants, both European and African, to come to America.

In the mid-1600s, planters in Virginia were given fifty acres of land for each person they brought to the colony. Anthony Johnson received 250 acres of land. He became a well-to-do Virginia landowner.

indentured servants. Many had finished their terms of indenture and were free. In fact, some free Africans bought land and had servants of their own. Africans were not enslaved by law until New Netherlands became New York in 1664.

Lerone Bennett, Jr., a well-known historian, has said the following about this period:

> *"In Virginia, then, as in other colonies, the first Negro settlers fell into a well established socioeconomic groove which carried with it no implications of racial inferiority. (This means they became part of a group that was already there and were not treated worse because they were African or because they were black.) For a period of forty years or more, the first Negroes accumulated land, voted, testified in court and mingled with whites on a basis of equality."*[1]

Slavery in the Colonies

About 250,000 enslaved Africans were living and working on Southern plantations by the mid-1700s. Until the mid-1660s, Africans in the colonies were indentured servants and free men and women. How could so many Africans become enslaved during the next 100 years? What was happening in the colonies to bring about a system of slavery?

The first Europeans who came to the Americas claimed the land they found. They did not own this land. It belonged to Native Americans, but the Europeans took it. They built farms, ran businesses, and governed towns that formed around their farms. At first, they paid for indentured servants to help with this work.

Certain crops would grow in the colonies that would not grow in Europe. Tobacco and cotton were two of them. The demand for these crops increased. The colonists' farms were enlarged to meet the demand. But the demand was too great. There were not enough indentured servants to work the farms.

Enslaved people transport cotton or tobacco from a plantation on the Savannah River to sell it for their "master."

[1] *Before the Mayflower*, Lerone Bennett, 1982

European slave traders began to get rich selling African slaves in America. The fact that they were selling humans did not seem to matter to them.

Colonial leaders quickly had to find more cheap labor. They might have used more indentured servants. They might have enslaved all their servants. They might have used a free-labor system that paid workers.

For a time, Native Americans were forced to work as slaves. Then some Europeans were made slaves. Convicts, prisoners of war, and people who had been kidnapped from the cities of Europe were forced to be servants for life in the colonies. This did not work because there were not enough of these people to meet the huge need for labor. Then Africans were enslaved.

How Africans Became Enslaved

Africa had been trading goods with Europe for hundreds of years before the slave trade began in the colonies. During that time, traders from Europe took the first guns to Africa. Once some African states acquired guns, others felt they needed guns to protect themselves. In exchange for guns, Europeans wanted African people to sell as slaves in the colonies.

The need for guns became so great in Africa that traders could demand many slaves in exchange for guns. This made the cost of slaves go way down. Soon, African slaves for life cost seven times less than indentured servants. There was not a large enough supply of English or Irish people who wanted to come or could be forced to come to the colonies. However, there seemed to be an endless supply of Africans.

 Some Africans exchanged prisoners from other tribes with Europeans for guns.

Africans who had come to the colonies as indentured servants had no contact with their home governments in Africa. Their governments could not protect them. Europeans did not have much respect for Africans. For example, Europeans knew little about the religions of African people. Most Europeans knew and respected only their own religions. Finally, European servants sometimes ran away. Because they where white, they blended in with other people in a new town or village. African people were more visible. You will find out more about how the change from servant to slave came about in Chapter 4.

 A free black man has been captured and is being led South to be sold as a slave.

ACTIVITY

WHY ENSLAVE AFRICAN PEOPLE?

Below are words that indicate why colonists chose Africans as the group of people to enslave. On a separate sheet of paper, match each word to a sentence in order to understand why this happened. Then write your own explanation of *why*.

1. MORE VISIBLE

    A. African governments did not know how Africans were being treated in the colonies.

2. LESS EXPENSIVE

    B. Europeans did not understand and value the cultures and religions of African people.

3. NOT PROTECTED

    C. There was a limited supply of people from Ireland and England who wanted to come to the colonies as indentured servants.

4. NOT RESPECTED

    D. Africans could be easily identified if they were trying to escape.

5. MORE PLENTIFUL

    E. Because of the gun trade, the same money that would buy an indentured servant for seven years would buy an African for life.

Write your answers on a separate piece of paper.

VOCABULARY TO KNOW

Use context clues or a dictionary to help you write definitions for the following words:

1. equality
2. status
3. value
4. visible
5. plentiful
6. respect
7. culture
8. origin

Thinking Critically

1. Name the three groups of people who were indentured servants in the English colonies between 1620 and 1660.

2. Explain why colonial leaders needed a fast source of labor that would not be costly in the early colonies.

3. List reasons why Africans were finally targeted for enslavement rather than Europeans or Native Americans.

Writing

4. Write a paragraph stating the position of a landowner against slavery in the early colonies. Give two reasons to support your position.

5. Draw a picture that shows how indentured servants of African and European origin worked and lived together between 1620 and 1660. Write a paragraph describing your picture.

4 AFRICANS AND THE SLAVE LAWS

1620-1750

 An African chief bargaining with European slave merchants for his prisoners of war. At first, Africans did not know the cruelty and harshness of what awaited enslaved people across the ocean.

This symbol originated in the Kinshasa, Congo and was created to look like a design on a wooden basket.

There was no slavery in the early Southern colonies. From 1620 to the 1660s, Africans who came to the colonies were indentured servants. Among the Africans were skilled farmers and artisans. In 1648, the governor of Virginia ordered the planting of rice. He did this on the advice of African farmers who told him that the climate and the soil of the colony, which was similar to that in their country, was good for rice.

ANTHONY JOHNSON, 250 acs. Northampton Co., 24 July 1651, ... At great Naswattock Cr., being a neck of land bounded on the S.W. by the maine Cr. & on S.E. & N.W. by two small branches issueing out of the mayne Cr. Trans. of 5 pers: Tho. Bemrose, Peter Bughhy, Antho. Cripps, Jno, Gesorroro, Richard Johnson.

Part of Anthony Johnson's deed to 250 acres of land in Virginia. Notice that the names of the five indentured servants he paid for are listed at the end of the deed.

Within three to seven years, many Africans had finished their terms of indenture. Some now owned land. Deeds in the 1650s in Virginia show that Africans owned hundreds of acres of land. Many also bought indentured servants. These servants were Europeans and Africans. Whether indentured or free, early African colonists were protected by the same laws as everyone else.

For more than forty years, Africans, Europeans and Native Americans were indentured servants. They made friendships. They married and had children. They lived and worked together. No group saw itself as better or worse than the other.

Slavery Becomes Legal

Colonial leaders who wanted a system of slavery used many ways to separate Europeans and Africans. The laws and ideas about Africans had to change before Africans could be set apart as slaves. At this time, England had a slave trade. Many colonists accepted slavery. They began to pass laws against Africans. In 1641, Massachusetts became the first colony to pass a slavery law. Other colonies soon passed similar laws. [1]

1 Next came Connecticut in 1650. Virginia followed in 1661 and Maryland in 1663. New York and New Jersey made a law allowing slavery in 1664.

Colonial leaders wrote laws to stop Europeans and Africans from living, working and marrying together. The colonial leaders used force against those who tried to keep their friendships. In Maryland, the right of an African to marry a non-African was outlawed in 1664. Soon other colonies passed laws against this, too. African people could no longer travel where they chose to go. Europeans could travel anywhere.

Churches were a part of this change, too. Some Africans became members of Christian church.[2] Most were not. Many church leaders taught that Europeans were superior because they were Christians. They used parts of the Bible to justify slavery. Many newspapers wrote stories in favor of slavery. They ran ads for slaves and runaway slaves.

GANG OF 25 SEA ISLAND COTTON AND RICE NEGROES,

By LOUIS D. DE SAUSSURE.

On *THURSDAY* the 25th Sept., 1852, at 11 o'clock, A.M., will be sold at RYAN'S MART, in Chalmers Street, in the City of Charleston,

A prime gang of 25 Negroes, accustomed to the culture of Sea Island Cotton and Rice.

CONDITIONS. —One-half Cash, balance by Bond, bearing interest from day of sale, payable in one and two years, to be secured by a mortgage of the negroes and approved personal security. Purchasers to pay for papers.

Newspapers supported slavery by printing advertisements for slave auctions and rewards for runaway slaves.

2 By 1641, there were forty African members of Bouweire Chapel, a Dutch church in New Amsterdam.

 Europeans held auctions to sell enslaved people to the highest bidder. Slaves were displayed on an auction block and priced according to their good health, strength, or ability to produce more slaves. Slaves were not considered human.

 Africans lost all their freedom when slavery was made legal. Their leisure often had to be part of their work. Here, African slaves are socializing while baling hay.

Skin Color Becomes Important

During the next 100 years, colonial leaders used skin color as a way to name groups. They used it to keep groups apart. Europeans were now called "white" people. Africans were called "black" people. Colonial leaders forced these two groups apart. They had a reason for this: they needed the indentured Europeans to help them keep Africans in slavery. By the mid-1700s, laws, religion and force were used to keep poor Europeans (now called "poor whites") separate and superior. This made it easier to bring about and enforce a system of slavery.

Poor whites began to see themselves in a different way because they had the same color as those in power. Some became overseers, or managers, of large plantations. Many worked toward becoming landowners themselves when their terms of indenture were over. Some became merchants. Africans now had few allies and most had lost their freedom.

 Colonial leaders gave poor whites power over Africans. This made the whites keep Africans in slavery. As overseers of plantations and landowners, poor whites began to think of themselves as superior to Africans.

 With the legalization of slavery, Africans had no chance of starting a life for themselves. They were enslaved for life, and their children would be, too.

ACTIVITY

> **ANTHONY JOHNSON**, 250 acs. Northampton Co., 24 July 1651, ... At great Naswattock Cr., being a neck of land bounded on the S.W. by the maine Cr. & on S.E. & N.W. by two small branches issueing out of the mayne Cr. Trans. of 5 pers: Tho. Bemrose, Peter Bughhy, Antho. Cripps, Jno, Gesorroro, Richard Johnson.

1. Translate the deed of Anthony Johnson into modern English. What did he deed? Explain.

2. Write a paragraph describing what the lives of the indentured servants might be like. Use facts as details to make your description more real.

Write your answers on a separate piece of paper.

VOCABULARY TO KNOW

Use context clues or a dictionary to help you write definitions for the following words:

1. superior
2. ally
3. justify
4. plantation

5. overseer
6. enforce
7. artisan
8. deed

Thinking Critically

1. Describe how the lives of African people changed when they could only be enslaved, not indentured people.

2. List three facts about early African colonial life.

3. Explain why colonial leaders separated indentured Africans from indentured Europeans.

Writing

4. List the ways that poor Europeans and Africans were turned against each other.

5. Consider how planters, merchants and government leaders tried to change ideas about African people. Write a paragraph explaining how this change helped to develop slavery.

6. Pretend you are an indentured European, an indentured African, a planter or a merchant living between 1620 and 1660. Tell a story about your life. Include any changes that would have affected your life during this period.

THE DREADED
MIDDLE PASSAGE

1650-1750

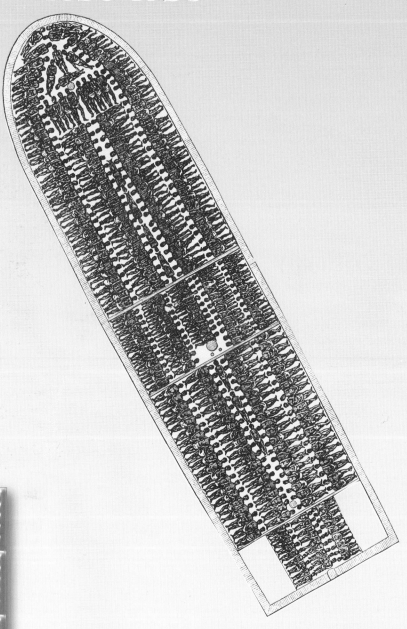

This symbol originated in Northern Senegal and was created to decorate cloth.

This diagram shows the lower deck of a slave ship. These ships were horribly overcrowded. Men, women and children were squeezed in and chained together by the legs and necks.

In Chapter 4, you learned how a legal system of American slavery in the colonies came about. Soon millions of African people were enslaved and brought to America. Historians call this time in history the Middle Passage. The following paragraphs describe what it was like to be brought to America to be a slave. This account was compiled from several sources.

By the mid-1700s, the largest group of people to settle in the American colonies were the English. People from the African continent were the second largest group. After 1650, colonists in the Southern colonies were looking for a source of forced labor to run their large farms. Most Africans who came to the colonies at this time were either traded for European goods or kidnapped in their country and then enslaved. They came from all levels of society. Some were farmers. Some were soldiers. Others were merchants, priests, princes or nobles.

The Middle Passage may be the cruelest part of the slave trade. The Middle Passage was the name given to the trip from Africa to the Americas on a slave ship. Ships carrying Africans were very overcrowded. Traders tried to make more money by packing the ship with more people.

GUSTAVUS VASA

Gustavus Vasa was born in Benin. (See map on page 4.) His real name was Olaudah Equiano. He spoke the Ibo language. In 1756, when he was eleven years old, he was kidnapped and taken by a slave ship to Virginia. For the next ten years, he had several "owners." One was a lieutenant in the English Navy. Another was an American Quaker. He learned several trades, including navigation, and earned enough money to buy his freedom in 1766. When Gustavus Vasa was forty-four, he wrote a book about his life in Benin and the horror of the Middle Passage. He wrote about his life in colonial America and the many other places where he traveled. He lived in England in the later years of his life and was a well-known abolitionist. He died in England in 1797.

Enslaved Africans were forced onto overcrowded slave ships during what was called the Middle Passage. Sometimes, enslaved people were thrown overboard or killed if they seemed rebellious or troublesome.

Men, women and children were squeezed into ships and chained together by the legs and the neck. The space where they lay was often no more than eighteen inches high. The people could barely move. Many people died from suffocation. Others became sick and died. Many wished they would die. People often tried to jump overboard. If caught, they were brutally whipped. Many times, the captives would mutiny against the captain and the crew.

African people who were kidnapped to be sold as slaves usually were separated from their families. The ship and the treatment they received were strange to them. Although slavery existed in Africa, [1] such treatment was not part of slavery. There was fear among the Africans that came from not knowing where they were being taken. The Middle Passage showed how cruel humans could be to each other. It was a taste of the life in slavery that was to come.

1   If you became a prisoner of war in African countries, you were often made a slave. As a slave, you became part of the community in which you lived. You had certain rights and would remain a slave only a set number of years, not for life. You might even marry a member of the group that you served. American slavery was much harsher. You had none of the rights of non-slaves. You were a slave for life, and your children were also slaves. You lost all hope of freedom.

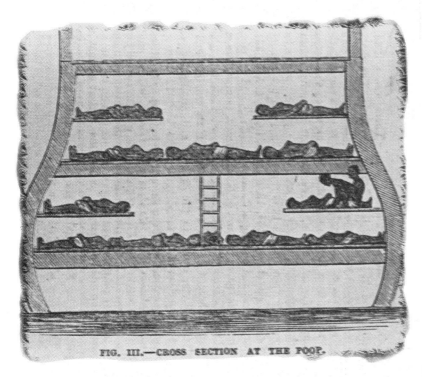

FIG. III.—CROSS SECTION AT THE POOP.

 The diagram to the left shows a cross-section of a slave ship. Most enslaved people barely had enough room to lie flat, while younger slaves sat crouched together to take up less room.

 Many times Africans would revolt against the captain and crew of slave ships in an attempt to regain their freedom.

ACTIVITY

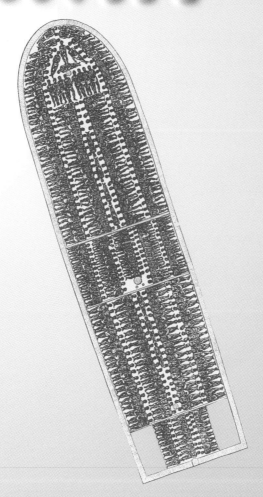

1. Reread the account of the Middle Passage in this chapter. Write a paragraph explaining why it is shocking to you.

2. Does the inhumane treatment in the Middle Passage ever happen in modern times? Explain your answer.

3. How can we prevent such inhumanity from happening? Write your thoughts as an essay, poem, speech, song, or other creative expression.

Write your answers on a separate piece of paper.

VOCABULARY TO KNOW

Use context clues or a dictionary to help you write definitions for the following words:

1. suffocation
2. mutiny
3. emotion

4. attitude
5. merchant
6. society

Thinking Critically

1. Describe the Middle Passage in your own words.

2. Different emotions and attitudes were a result of are the Middle Passage. Emotions and attitudes could include anger, fear, sadness, shock, disgust, shame, sympathy, pain, confusion or their opposites. List the emotions and attitudes you think different people might have felt at the time of the Middle Passage.

Writing

3. Pretend that you are a prisoner on a slave ship bound for America in 1700. You are thinking about how you would tell your mother or father, if you ever see them again, what is happening to you. Prepare a speech for the class in which you tell them your thoughts.

6 AFRICANS IN THE AMERICAN REVOLUTION

1770-1776

 The Boston Massacre was one of the events that led to the Revolutionary War. On March 5, 1770, Crispus Attucks was the first man to die in the fight for freedom. He was an African American.

This symbol originated in Northern Senegal and was created to decorate cloth.

At first, Native American, African and European servants made up the labor force of the colonies. Europeans and Africans worked and lived as equals in the early American colonies. As the colonies began to grow, there was a problem getting enough labor to clear land, build homes and grow crops. As long as labor could be gotten at very little cost, colonial leaders did not care about the color or national origin of the work force.

As colonists began to grow a wide variety of crops for trade, there was a need for more labor. The rise of large plantations to meet the great demand for products such as sugar, tobacco and cotton led to the decision to set up a system of slavery.

By 1700, the process of slavery was well established in the colonies. When the American Revolution began, there were more enslaved people than free people in many areas of the South.

The Boston Massacre

In the latter part of the 1700s, the British colonies in America began to rebel against British rule. On March 5, 1770, an incident that is now called the *Boston Massacre* occurred. A few African men were among the group of townspeople who attacked several British soldiers. The British soldiers fired into the crowd, killing three men and wounding eight. Crispus Attucks, a formerly enslaved and now free man, was the first to die. He had escaped from his "master" in Framingham, Massachusetts, about twenty years earlier. On the night of the massacre, he led a group of townspeople against the soldiers. When the first shots were fired, he fell.

 Crispus Attucks led townspeople in an attack on British soldiers. He was the first to die in the Boston Massacre.

Africans in the Revolution

The Boston Massacre and the actions that followed led to the Revolutionary War. African men were a part of many of the events that led to the war. They believed in freedom for all. For example, they were among the Minutemen alerted by Paul Revere during his ride through Massachusetts. They fought in the early battles and in the major battles of the war. Peter Salem and Salem Poor became heroes in the Battle of Bunker Hill. Cuff Hayes, Prince Hall and Cesar Dickerson were a few of many brave soldiers who fought during the revolutionary period. Pompey, an African American spy, gathered information which led to the victory at Stony Point. Crossing the Delaware with George Washington were two African Americans, Oliver Cromwell and Prince Whipple.

The Declaration of Independence was written to convince American colonists to fight for their freedom from Britain. Its writing was mainly the work of Thomas Jefferson. The Declaration of Independence was adopted in 1776. The document stated the idea that "all men are created equal." It further stated that every man had rights that could not be taken away. These rights included "life, liberty and the pursuit of happiness."

The Declaration of Independence also had a clause about slavery. In harsh words, it said that the King of England was taking away the life and liberty of men through slavery. He was blamed for the increase of the slave trade and for carrying human beings into bondage to a distant land. Although it spoke only about the King of England, the Declaration of Independence said that slavery was wrong. Slave owners did not like this clause. They did not want these ideas in the final writing of the document. They threatened not to join the Union. The clause against slavery was removed from the Declaration of Independence.

Africans played a major role in many events during the American Revolution. When George Washington crossed the Delaware, he was accompanied by Oliver Cromwell and Prince Whipple.

Some Africans Fight for Britain, Some for the Colonies

When the Revolutionary War began in 1775, the British recruited enslaved African men. They promised them freedom if they would join in the fight against the colonies. Thousands of enslaved African men escaped and joined the British forces. Some served as laborers, carpenters or blacksmiths. Others were spies or fought as soldiers and sailors. After the war, thousands of African men left this country on British ships as free men.

At the same time, Africans were also fighting on the side of the colonists. In 1775, however, when George Washington was placed in charge of colonial troops, he said that these men could no longer be soldiers. Some white men objected to African men having guns. Also, they knew that when African men fought for "white freedom," they would want freedom for their own people even more.

In 1776, George Washington was forced to change his mind. The colonial army badly needed more soldiers. The only way Rhode Island could make up its quota of soldiers was to enlist African men. Many African men, free and enslaved, were joining the British side. Washington at first allowed free African men who had fought in the early battles of the war to enlist. Later, all African men, enslaved and free, were welcomed. Some Africans fought in place of their "masters." Some fought because they were promised freedom. Others were free and fought because they believed in what the colonists were fighting for.

At first, African men were not used as fighting soldiers, but as laborers. Then they were allowed to fight, mostly in integrated units alongside Europeans. As many as 5,000 African men fought in the Revolutionary War. They helped to win American freedom.

Eventually, George Washington realized that he needed the help of African soldiers to win the Revolution. These African Americans are fighting on the side of the colonists.

Slavery After the War

After the Revolutionary War, Americans began to look again at the question of enslaving people. They had won freedom from England. They now enjoyed the rights of the Declaration of Independence. Yet many Africans, who had helped fight for that freedom, were still enslaved. Some white colonists believed it was hypocritical to have fought for freedom and still hold people in a system of slavery. Many of these slave owners granted freedom to their slaves. Other African men were granted freedom for their bravery during the war. Thousands of other enslaved Africans escaped to freedom.

Many African leaders worked together to end slavery and unequal treatment for free African Americans. Absalom Jones was co-founder of the Free African Society in 1787 in Philadelphia. This was a church, a mutual aid society and a political group. In 1794, part of this group helped Reverend Jones found one of the first African churches in the North, the African Episcopal Church. Absalom Jones was also a protest leader. In 1800, he was part of a group of free African men who filed an anti-slavery petition in Congress.

In 1787, the Constitutional Convention met in Philadelphia. The issue of slavery in the colonies was again discussed. The framers of the Constitution agreed that by January 1, 1808, the slave trade would end. After 1808, no more slaves could be brought into the country. However, Africans already in the United States and their descendants would remain enslaved for life.

In 1787, the Constitutional Convention was held at Independence Hall in Philadelphia.

 Large numbers of slaves crossed Union lines as the bluecoats pushed into the South. As slaves left plantations and fled to the Union soldiers, the South suffered economically. The South was hurt because it had depended on slave labor.

ACTIVITY

**AMERICA'S FIRST AFRICAN MASON
DISCUSSES DISCRIMINATION**

The following first-person account is taken from Eyewitness:
The Negro in American History, by William L. Katz, Pitman
Publishers, 1964:

. . . Patience I say, for were we not possessed of a great
measure of it you could not bear up under the daily insults
you meet with in the streets of Boston; much more on public
days of recreation, how are you shamefully abus'd, and that at
such a degree, that you may be truly said to carry your lives in
your hands . . . [since many have been attacked] by a mob of
shame-less, low-lived, envious, spiteful persons, some of them
not long since, servants in gentlemen's kitchens . . . .

My brethren, let us not be cast down under these and
many abuses we at present labour under: for the darkest is
before the break of day . . . .

Although you are deprived of the means of education;
yet you are not deprived of the means of meditation **1**

Prince Hall

Prince Hall was an African leader of the
Revolutionary War period. He fought in
the Revolutionary War. He founded the
world's first Masonic Lodge for persons
of African descent. He also organized a
group of African men in Boston to send
a petition to Congress against
enslavement. He used America's legal
system to seek an end to slavery and to
gain equal treatment for African
Americans.

1. Write a modern version of what
Prince Hall said.

2. Imagine that you lived when
Prince Hall did. Write your own
advice to enslaved Africans.

1 Prince Hall, *A Charged Delivered to the African Lodge*, June
24, 1797, pp. 10-13.

Write your answers on a separate piece of paper.

VOCABULARY TO KNOW

Use context clues or a dictionary to help you write definitions for the following words:

1. **bondage**
2. **quota**
3. **document**
4. **integrate**
5. **framer**
6. **hypocrisy**

Thinking Critically

1. List some of the early battles that African Americans took part in before George Washington was in charge of the Army.

2. George Washington finally decided to allow African men to enlist in the colonial Army. Explain the reasons for his decision.

Writing

3. In your own words, explain how African Americans were part of the Revolutionary War.

4. Is it wrong to fight for freedom and to also hold another person enslaved? Explain your position.

5. Pretend you are one of the many African American soldiers who fought at the Battle of Bunker Hill in June 1776. It is July 1775, and George Washington has just ordered that no African American man can enlist in the colonial army. You are a free man, but many of your relatives and friends are enslaved. Write a letter to George Washington explaining how African Americans have already helped the colonial side. Include your feelings about the hypocrisy of a country fighting for freedom, yet practicing slavery. Explain why African Americans will fight bravely for freedom.

6. After discussing with your class the first-person account in this chapter, tell how you think the author felt about his situation.

THE BRUTALITY OF SLAVERY

1790-1850

 Enslaved people were often whipped, or lashed, as a form of punishment. Sometimes white "masters" forced other slaves to administer this punishment.

This symbol originated in South Africa and was created to look like a Zulu wood carving.

Large numbers of enslaved Africans were forced to live and to work on big plantations. What was daily life on a large plantation like for enslaved people?

Read the account of enslavement and plantation life below.

"A slave was thought to be property that could be bought and sold like any other piece of property. Whole families were separated in slave sales: husband from wife, sister from brother, and even mother from child. A slave served only one "master," but could be abused by any white person. Enslaved people had to obey many rules. They could not be taught to read or write. Slaves could not have books. Slaves could not gather in large groups. They could not work with or marry free African people.

"Punishment for breaking slave laws took many forms. The most common was being whipped with a lash. Persons with easier jobs who broke slave rules were forced to do hard work in the fields. Food rations were cut. Some were put in jail, in chains, or in irons. Many were branded, tortured or mutilated. Slavery was constant hard work. Most slaves worked in the fields. Slaves described their workdays as lasting from 'can- see' (dawn) to 'can't-see' (dusk). After field work there were other chores to do, such as mending fences and roads. It was usually late in the day before they could eat their first hot meal. This kind of work went on for six days a week, every week of the year."

Other enslaved Africans worked as servants inside the master's house. They often had easier lives than those in the fields. But they, too, worked all day, six days a week. House slaves had to cook, clean, weave, sew, mend and nurse.

ELIZABETH KECKLEY

Elizabeth Keckley was born in 1818. As a young woman, she lived as a slave on a large plantation. She hoped for freedom and a better way of life. After learning the dressmaking trade, she did extra jobs to earn money and was able to buy her freedom. Miss Keckley moved to Washington, D.C., and set up a dressmaking business. Mrs. Abraham Lincoln became one of her many customers. Mrs. Lincoln asked Miss Keckley to work at the White House. In 1868, Elizabeth Keckley wrote a book called Behind the Scenes. It was about life in the White House.

Enslaved African men and women were also skilled crafts workers. Many were carpenters, masons, blacksmiths, potters and silversmiths. Many Africans brought other skills with them from their native countries, for example, some came with medical skills. They knew how to treat different illnesses. They became doctors for others who were enslaved. At times, their cures would be used by their masters.

Slaves usually ate the same plain food day after day. Pork and corn meal were most common. Clothes were old and patched. Enslaved people had shoes only in winter. Slave quarters were little more than shacks that did not keep out the rain and cold.

Life in slavery was harsh and cruel. Yet when the master and the overseer were not around, enslaved people tried to build a positive and joyful community life to balance the horrors of slavery. They continued to hope for freedom and a better life for themselves and for their children.

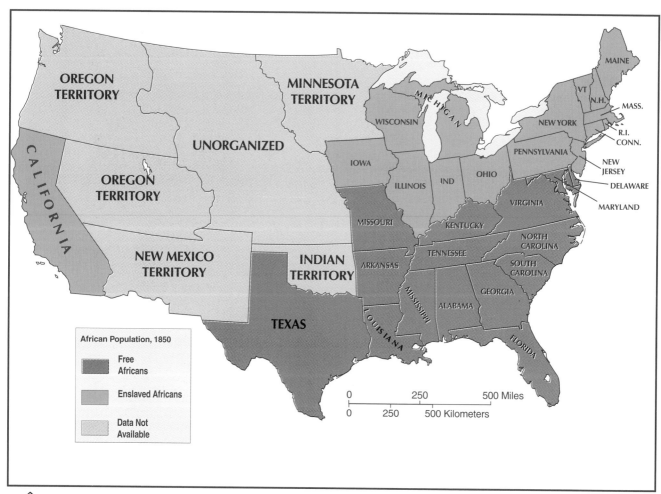

 Free versus enslaved African American population, 1850

 Because whites feared a slave revolt, they accused two enslaved Africans. The Africans were innocent. They were burned at the stake in New York City in 1741.

ACTIVITY CHART

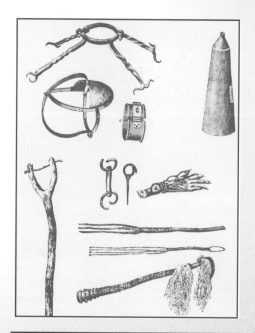

When you think of slavery, you may think about large plantations in the South. Your thinking may come from television, books or from movies. You may not know that not all Africans who came to this country were enslaved. Those who were enslaved did not all work on plantations. Some worked on small farms. Many worked in cities.

AFRICAN PEOPLE–FREE AND ENSLAVED				
	1790		1850	
STATE	FREE	ENSLAVED	FREE	ENSLAVED
North Carolina	5,418	100,572	27,452	288,548
Georgia	736	29,264	3,318	385,000
South Carolina	1,906	107,094	9,016	384,984
New York	4,676	21,324	41,000	0
Pennsylvania	6,263	3,737	54,000	0
Virginia	12,573	293,427	54,472	472,528

1. Look at the chart above to see how many African people were enslaved and how many were free in 1790 and in 1850.

2. On a separate sheet of paper, add the free and enslaved columns together to get the total African population of each state in 1790 and in 1850. Then find the percentages of free and enslaved Africans for each state. Compare the states by listing them in order from the highest to the lowest percentage of free and enslaved for both years. Notice the change in percents over the 60-year period.

ACTIVITY

PIE CHART

SLAVE HOLDERS IN THE U.S. IN 1850

The pie graph below shows the percent of slaveholders and the number of slaves they "owned." Two percent of all slaveholders each owned large numbers of slaves. (See page 54.)

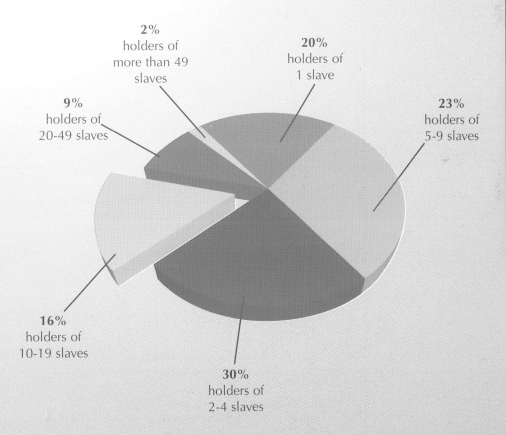

2%
holders of
more than 49
slaves

20%
holders of
1 slave

9%
holders of
20-49 slaves

23%
holders of
5-9 slaves

16%
holders of
10-19 slaves

30%
holders of
2-4 slaves

1. On a separate paper, practice putting the information in the pie chart into another graphic form. You may create a chart, a line graph, a bar graph, or another graphic.

ACTIVITY

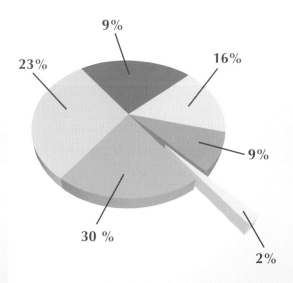

9%

23%

16%

9%

30 %

2%

1. Two percent of slave holders had more than forty-nine slaves. The chart below lists the five groups that make up this 2%.

	Number of Slaves	Number of Slaveholders
1.	50-99	6,196
2.	100-199	1479
3.	200-299	187
4.	300-499	56
5.	500 or more	11

2. As you can see from the pie chart, the largest group of slaveholders (30%) owned 2-4 slaves. The smallest group of slaveholders owned the largest number of slaves each. What does this tell you about the economics of the South? Were most people able to buy slaves? Who probably controlled most of the money?

Write your answers on a separate piece of paper.

VOCABULARY TO KNOW

Use context clues or a dictionary to help you write definitions for the following words:

1. abuse
2. mutilate

3. blacksmith
4. mason

Thinking Critically

1. What does this chapter tell you about the life as an enslaved person? Make a list of the kinds of work done by enslaved people. Make a second list of words that describe the living conditions of enslaved people.

2. Study the chart, "African People: Free and Enslaved," on page 52. List all the information that is different from what you already knew. (For example, did you know that New York State had slavery, or that a southern state such as Virginia had as many as 64,472 free African Americans in 1850, well before the Civil War? Were you surprised? Explain.

Writing

3. Think of yourself as an enslaved person on a large plantation. Use the information from your lists to describe a typical day on the plantation.

4. Photocopy an account on the institution of slavery from a library book. In a paragraph, explain from whose point of view it is written (enslaved person or slave owner) and what it tells about life as an enslaved person.

CHAPTER 8

SLAVE REBELLIONS
1820-1865

 In July of 1839, Don Jose Ruiz and Don Pedro Montez of the Island of Cuba purchased fifty-three African slaves in Havana. They forced them aboard the *Amistad* to transport them to Principe, Cuba. Four days into the trip, the Africans revolted. Sengbe was their leader. He armed them with captors. They tried to sail back to their African homeland, but a U.S. ship arrested them. They were jailed in the U.S. and tried. Their legal battle was long and went to the Supreme Court, but they won their freedom. They returned home to West Africa in 1841.

This symbol originated in Eastern Nigeria and was created to look like a plaited prayer mat design.

From what you know about slavery, do you think that African Americans who were enslaved accepted their lives in slavery without protest? If they didn't accept their enslaved lives, how do you think they fought against slavery?

Lerone Bennett, Jr., a well-known historian, tells us this:

> "The masses who appeared to be obedient waged a day-to-day resistance to slavery. They worked no harder than they had to; put on deliberate slow-downs; staged sit-down strikes; set fires to buildings and fields; broke tools; and trampled crops. At times, slave owners were quietly poisoned by their slaves." [1]

 Some enslaved Africans found freedom through revolts and escape.

Another account tells us that many African Americans tried to escape. Some kept trying until they did.

> "Escaped slaves banded together. Some formed colonies in the forests and boldly attacked plantations, cities and towns. In August, 1831, in Southampton, Virginia, a quiet and trusted slave rose in rebellion. Nat Turner and a band of followers began by killing sixty or more whites. Turner's rebellion was followed by many more. In 1822, a plot by Denmark Vesey, a free man, was discovered. Another slave revealed his plan of insurrection which would have involved thousands of slaves" [2]

 Two months after his revolt, Nat Turner was captured and hanged, but his rebellion caused debates all over the country about how to end slavery.

1 *Before the Mayflower*, Lerone Bennett, 1982

2 *United States and its Neighbors*, Silver Burdett Co., 1982

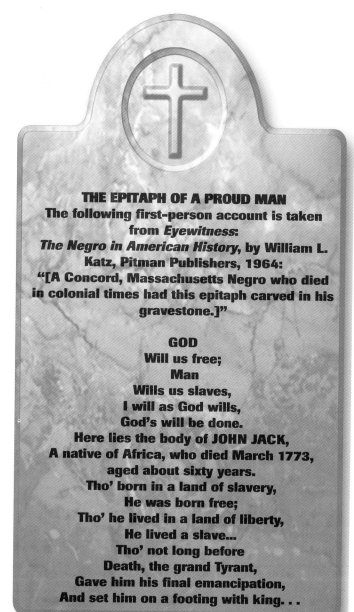

THE EPITAPH OF A PROUD MAN
The following first-person account is taken from *Eyewitness:*
The Negro in American History, by William L. Katz, Pitman Publishers, 1964:
"[A Concord, Massachusetts Negro who died in colonial times had this epitaph carved in his gravestone.]"

GOD
Will us free;
Man
Wills us slaves,
I will as God wills,
God's will be done.
Here lies the body of JOHN JACK,
A native of Africa, who died March 1773,
aged about sixty years.
Tho' born in a land of slavery,
He was born free;
Tho' he lived in a land of liberty,
He lived a slave...
Tho' not long before
Death, the grand Tyrant,
Gave him his final emancipation,
And set him on a footing with king. . .

JOSEPH CINQUE

Joseph Cinque was a rice planter from the Mende nation of West Africa. His real name was Sengbe. He was kidnapped in 1839 and sent to Havana, Cuba, on a slave ship. From Havana, Sengbe, forty-nine men and three children were sent to another Cuban town on a ship called the *Amistad*. During the trip, he led fifty four men in a revolt and seized the ship. He said: ". . . I could die happy if by dying I could save so many of my brothers from the bondage of the white man." Cinque and his men tried to sail back to Africa but were captured by a U.S. Coast Guard ship and put in a U.S. prison. After a long court battle, they were freed by the Supreme Court of the United States. Ex-President John Quincy Adams was their lawyer. Sengbe and thirty-five others returned home to West Africa in 1841.

African Resistance

The revolts of Nat Turner and Denmark Vesey are only two of the better-known slave revolts. But there were many rebellions and they began as soon as African captives were taken onto slave ships. A few attempts to take over slave ships were successful. Often, Africans resisted becoming enslaved by jumping overboard. Some starved themselves or killed themselves in other ways. Once in the Americas, resistance continued. Some enslaved Africans ran away. Others organized revolts.

The first revolt occurred in 1526 in a Spanish settlement in what is now South Carolina. There were 500 Spaniards and 100 enslaved Africans. After the revolt, the Spaniards went back to Haiti. The Africans stayed on to be the first permanent settlers other than the Native Americans in North America.

In some cases, Africans and Native Americans joined together in revolt. One such uprising took place in Hartford, Connecticut, in 1657. Throughout the next 200 years, there were at least 250 more revolts.[3]

African Americans, enslaved and free, rebelled against enslavement in many ways. Some freedom fighters filed petitions against slavery in the courts. Others started anti-slavery groups. Some wrote books and pamphlets and made speeches. African American men and women helped others to escape. These people used whatever power and strength they had. They never stopped rebelling against slavery.

African and Native Americans sometimes joined forces to revolt against Europeans.

[3] *Before the Mayflower*, Lerone Bennett, 1982

On Christmas Eve, 1855, a group of teenage boys and girls escaped by wagon from Virginia. Their leader's name was Ann Wood. When a posse surrounded them, she dared the whites to fire. She was holding a double-barreled pistol in one hand and a long knife in the other hand. The posse retreated and the proud young people reached Philadelphia in safety.

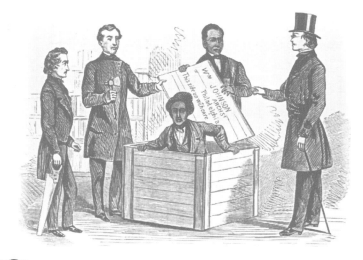

Henry Brown worked in a tobacco factory in Richmond, Virginia. He planned a different way to escape enslavement. He asked a white friend to seal him in a box and ship him to Philadelphia. When the box was opened, Brown stepped out and sang: "I waited patiently for the Lord, and He heard my prayer."

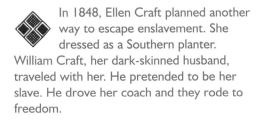

In 1848, Ellen Craft planned another way to escape enslavement. She dressed as a Southern planter. William Craft, her dark-skinned husband, traveled with her. He pretended to be her slave. He drove her coach and they rode to freedom.

ACTIVITY

THE DREAM OF LIBERTY AND PEACE

The following first-person account is taken from **Eyewitness**: *The Negro in American History* by William L. Katz, Pitman Publishers, 1964:

"[What are the thoughts of a slave as he plans escape? Lewis Clarke, a Kentucky slave in the 1840s, tells the worries and fears that went through his mind when he was about to make a break for freedom. Clarke made his escape a good one.]"

I had long thought and dreamed of LIBERTY; I was now determined to make an effort to gain it. No tongue can tell the doubt, the perplexities, the anxiety, which a slave feels when making up his mind upon this subject. If he makes an effort and is not successful, he must be laughed at by his fellows, he will be beaten unmercifully by the master, and then watched and used the harder for it all his life.

And then, if he gets away, who, what, will he find? He is ignorant of the world. All the white part of mankind that he has ever seen are enemies to him and all his kind. How can he venture where none but white faces shall greet him? The master tells him that abolitionists decoy slaves off into the free states to catch them and sell them to Louisiana or Mississippi; and, if he goes to Canada, the British will put him in a mine underground, with both eyes put out, for life. How does he know what or whom to believe? A horror of great darkness comes upon him, as he thinks over what might befall him. Long, very long time did I think of escaping before I made the effort.

At length the report was started that I was to be sold for Louisiana. Then I thought it was time to act. My mind was made up.

On a separate piece of paper, write your opinion of how slavery made enslaved people feel. Tell what choices you think they had.

ACTIVITY

THE DREAM OF LIBERTY AND PEACE

The following first-person account is taken from *Early African-American Classics*, edited by Anthony Appiah, Bantam, 1990, from *Incidents in the Life of a Slave Girl*, by Harriett Jacobs, edited by L. Maria Child, and written in 1861:

CHILDHOOD

I was born a slave; but I never knew it till six years of happy childhood had passed away. My father was a carpenter, and considered so intelligent and skillful in his trade, that, when buildings out of the common line were to be erected, he was sent for from long distances, to be head workman...His strongest wish was to purchase his children; but, though he several times offered his hard earnings for that purpose he never succeeded...though we were all slaves, I was so fondly shielded that I never dreamed I was a piece of merchandise, trusted to them for safe keeping, and liable to be demanded of them at any moment...I had also a great treasure in my maternal grandmother, who was a remarkable woman in many respects. She was the daughter of a planter in South Carolina, who, at his death, left her mother and his three children free, with money to go to St. Augustine, where they had relatives. It was during the Revolutionary War; and they were captured on their passage, carried back, and sold to different purchasers. Such was the story my grandmother used to tell me; but I do not remember all the particulars. She was a little girl when she was captured and sold to the keeper of a large hotel. I have often heard her tell how hard she fared during childhood.

On a separate piece of paper, write the story Harriett's grandmother might have told her. Use your knowledge of the lives of enslaved people at this time. Share your story with the class.

Write your answers on a separate piece of paper.

VOCABULARY TO KNOW

Use context clues or a dictionary to help you write definitions for the following words:

1. **resistance**
2. **insurrection**
3. **petition**
4. **protest**
5. **rebellion**
6. **revolt**

Thinking Critically

1. List some of the different forms of rebellion against slavery in America.

2. Describe day-to-day resistance to enslavement by the of slaves.

Writing

3. Write a report about the rebellion of Nat Turner or Denmark Vesey. Use the library to find more information.

4. Pretend that you are enslaved on a large plantation. Tell what you would do to rebel against enslavement and what the result might be.

AFRICAN AMERICANS IN THE WESTWARD EXPANSION

1840-1900

 During the western movement, all races, creeds and colors moved their families west for hope of a better life as shown in the engraving above called "The Homesteader."

This symbol originated in Eastern Nigeria and was created to look like an Igbo painted wall pattern.

The westward movement in America appealed to people of all races, creeds and colors. Except for Native Americans whose land was taken away, people on the frontier were more equal. On the frontier, people were more often judged by their skills than by their color or national origin. Cooperation was needed to build homes, grow crops, hunt for food and stay alive.

The skills and life experiences of African men and women were a vital part of the European development of the West before the Civil War.[1] Many enslaved people went west in different ways. They walked behind the covered wagons. They tended the "master's" cattle. They went ahead in search of water or game. They did whatever tasks were needed on the journey. They cleared the fields, built cabins, planted crops and branded cattle.

Other African Americans went west as free persons. Some were missionaries. John Marrant of New York worked with the Cherokees and the Creeks. John Stewart, a Baptist minister from Virginia, worked with the Wyandot nation. Others were inn-keepers, trappers, miners and farmers. Still others went to seek adventure. They worked to build the railroads. They became cowhands and riders with the Pony Express.

Free African American men, such as Greenbury Logan, helped to settle Texas. He and many other African American men fought for Texan independence from Mexico. Many African Americans were at the Alamo. George William Bush was a leading pioneer and a settler of Oregon and Washington State. Alexander Leidesdorff went to California in 1841. He brought the first steamboat as well as the first race horse to California. He built San Francisco's first hotel. Thousands of African Americans were among the "forty-niners" in the California gold rush. Men such as Alvin Coffey became wealthy. African women made their marks, too. Mary Ellen Pleasant got rich speculating on the California gold rush. In 1850, the richest African American population lived in California.

 African American Alexander Leidesdorff was responsible for building San Fransisco's first hotel.

---

[1] "Developing the West" here means the European development of farms, towns, cities and states, as different from the centuries of development of many nations of Native Americans before this time.

IN OUR OWN IMAGE

Africans and Native Americans Cooperate

African Americans who went westward often related well to Native Americans. Both saw white Americans as enemies. Both shared common problems and often cooperated with each other. Escaped slaves sought refuge with Native American nations around the country. They adopted Native American ways. Some became leaders.

James Beckwourth escaped enslavement and was adopted by the Crow nation. He later became their chief. In 1850, he found a pass through

 James Beckwourth found freedom as a member of the Crow Indian tribe. The route he discovered through the Sierra Nevada Mountains became an important path for Americans looking for gold during the Gold Rush.

 An African named York helped Lewis and Clark on their expedition to explore the Louisiana Territory. York acted as an interperetor between the Native Americans and the expedition.

the Sierra Nevada mountains. The pass, named after Beckwourth, was an important route to California during the gold rush. In 1804, an enslaved man named York was of great help to the Lewis and Clark Expedition. Along with Sacajawea, a Native American woman, he acted as an interpreter and a guide in exploring the Louisiana Territory.

The West: Slave or Free?

African Americans who went westward often did not have citizenship or equal rights, including the right to vote. Most western states passed laws to limit what African American people could do in their state. To enter Iowa in 1839, African people had to put up a $500 bond per person and prove their freedom legally. Most African American people had neither the money nor the proof needed to enter Iowa.

Western states did not want slavery. Abraham Lincoln said that the new land must be kept "for homes of free white people. This cannot be, to any considerable extent, if slavery shall be planted with them. These "free white people" thought that slavery would take away jobs and land that should be for them." But Southern landowners wanted to expand slavery to the new land in the West. They wanted to keep the plantation system and slavery. These opposite views led to arguments and fighting.

The final compromise reached over Missouri and California is explained in Chapter 11. In Kansas, there was bloody fighting about whether or not to have slavery. Slavery existed in Kansas, but Kansas entered the Union as a free state in 1861. Thousands of African Americans went west after the Civil War. Most were very poor and searched for a better way of life. Some were soldiers, business people and politicians. Others were farmers and cowhands. These cowhands were among the "good" and "bad" guys in the new Western towns.

Nat Love, called "Deadwood Dick," rode with Billy the Kid, Jesse James and Bat Masterson. Isiah Dorman rode and died with General Custer in the battle at Little Big Horn.

 Nat Love, "Deadwood Dick," rode the West with Billy The Kid (top) and Jesse James (bottom). Love said his two friends were "misunderstood" men, not criminals.

 Many African Americans went West in search of better opportunities. This man was a gold miner in Auburn Ravine, California 1852, during the Gold Rush.

IN OUR OWN IMAGE

 Alvin Coffey was one of many talented craftspeople who went west during the Gold Rush. He panned for gold and worked as a cobbler. He earned enough money to buy his enslaved family's freedom. He also bought a farm in California. Later in his life, Alvin became wealthy.

The Peoples Party

In the 1880s, white farmers joined together to try to save their farms. After the Civil War, farmers were paid very low prices for their crops. Many could not pay their bills. Many farmers were losing their farms and homes to creditors. By the 1880s, some European American farmers saw that they would be a much stronger group if African American farmers joined them. They formed a Farmer's Alliance which tried to save their farms.

The Farmer's Alliance led to the formation of a political party called the People's or Populist Party. It fought for a secret unbiased ballot, an end to prison chain gangs, and for laws to help farmers. For a few years, the Populists helped to elect many African American officials. The most famous was George H. White. He was a member of Congress from 1896 to 1900.

Many leaders in the North and South did not want African Americans and European Americans to work together. They feared that together these groups might elect leaders who would pass laws to take away the unfair power of landowners. This fear contributed to the death of the Populist party. African Americans had already played an important part in developing the West. By the 1900s, they were working with European Americans to bring more equality to all people in the West.

GEORGE HENRY WHITE

George Henry White was a Congressman from North Carolina from 1897 to 1901. He sponsored America's first anti-lynching bill in Congress. He fought against discrimination in every way he could. One day in Congress he asked his fellow Congressmen: "How long will you sit in your seats and hear and see the principles that underlie the foundations of this government sapped away little by little?"

 General Custer became well-known for the battle of Little Big Horn during the Civil War, in which he was killed as he fought to take away land from the Sioux.

ACTIVITY

A FORTY-NINER MAKES A NEW LIFE IN CALIFORNIA

The following first-person account is taken from *Eyewitness: The Negro in American History*, by William L. Katz, Pitman Publishers, 1964:

[After Alvin Coffey and his master came to California during the Gold Rush, the master took away both the $5,000 which Coffey had earned for him in the mines and the $700 which the slave had earned for himself working nights. Then he sold the slave to a new master. Coffey convinced his new owner that he could earn enough in the mines to buy his freedom as well as the freedom of his wife and three children. The master agreed, and by 1860, Coffey's family were all with him, free and prosperous in Tehama County—and one of the noted pioneer families of California. Here is his own story of his first trip westward.]

I started from St. Louis, Missouri, on the 2nd of April in 1849. There was quite a crowd of neighbors who drove through the mud and rain to St. Joe to see us off. About the first of May we organized the train. There were twenty wagons in number and from three to five men to each wagon. We crossed the Missouri River at Savanna Landing on or about the 6th, no, the 1st week in May. . . . At six in the morning, there were three more went to relieve those on guard. One of the three that came in had cholera so bad that he was in lots of misery. Dr. Bassett, the captain of the train, did all he could for him, but he died at 10 o'clock and we buried him. We got ready and started at 11 the same day and the moon was new just then.

We got news every day that people were dying by the hundreds in St. Joe and St. Louis. It was alarming. When we hitched up and got ready to move, [the] Dr. said, "Boys, we will have to drive day and night.". . . We drove night and day and got out of reach of the cholera. . . .

We got across the plains to Fort Laramie, the 16th of June and the ignorant driver broke down a good many oxen on the trains. There were a good many ahead of us, who had doubled up their trains and left tons upon tons of bacon and other provisions. . . .

Starting to cross the desert to Black Rock at 4 o'clock in the evening, we traveled all night. The next day it was hot and sandy. . . .

A great number of cattle perished before we got to Black Rock. . . . I drove our oxen all the time and I knew about how much an ox could stand. Between nine and ten o'clock a breeze came up and the oxen threw up their heads and seemed to have new life. At noon, we drove into Black Rock. . . .

We crossed the South Pass on the Fourth of July. The ice next morning was as thick as a dinner plate.

Write a short story or play about Alvin Coffey. You may wish to work with a group to create your presentation and perform it for your class.

ACTIVITY

Nat Love won the title of "Deadwood Dick" at an 1876 rodeo.

NAT LOVE, "DEADWOOD DICK," COWBOY

The following first-person account is taken from: *Eyewitness: The Negro in American History*, by William L. Katz, Pitman Publishers, 1964:

"**[A few years after the Civil War, Nat Love, fifteen years old and a former slave, rode West seeking new adventure. He found it and wrote about it in *The Life and Adventures of Nat Love*, published in 1907. His boastful tales are as believable as those told by Davy Crockett, Daniel Boone, Jim Beckwourth, and earlier Western hands and tall-tale spinners. Nat Love tells how he won the title of "Deadwood Dick" on July 4, 1876 in Deadwood City.]**

...Our trail boss was chosen to pick out the mustangs from a herd of wild horses just off the range, and he picked out twelve of the most wild and vicious horses that he could find.

The conditions of the contest were that each of us who were mounted was to rope, throw, tie, bridle and saddle, and mount the particular horse picked for us in the shortest time possible. The man accomplishing the feat in the quickest time [was] to be declared the winner.

It seems to me that the horse chosen for me was the most vicious of the lot. Everything being in readiness, the "45" cracked and we all sprang forward together, each of us making for our particular mustang.

I roped, threw, tied, bridled, saddled, and mounted my mustang exactly nine minutes from the crack of the gun. The time of the next nearest competitor was twelve minutes and thirty seconds. This gave me the record and championship of the West, which I held up to the time I quit the business in 1880, and my record has never been beaten. It is worthy of passing remark that I never had a horse pitch with me so much as that mustang, but I never stopped sticking my spurs in him and using my quirt on his flanks until I proved his master. Right there the assembled crowd named me Deadwood Dick and proclaimed me champion roper of the western cattle country.

Make a chart with three columns.

Topics to Compare	How like reality?	How different from reality?

Under "Topics to Compare," list topics about the West and cowhands that you picked up from the movies and television. Then, in the other two columns, compare what you have learned from this book, movies and television and their relation to reality.

CHAPTER 9 REVIEW

Write your answers on a separate piece of paper.

VOCABULARY TO KNOW

Use context clues or a dictionary to help you write
definitions for the following words:

1. creed
2. refuge
3. bond

4. compromise
5. political party
6. interpreter

Thinking Critically

1. List several contributions of African Americans who went west during the 1800s.

2. Explain why western states did not want slavery.

Writing

3. Write a biography of one of the following men: James Beckwourth, Alexander Leidesdorff, "Deadwood Dick," Alvin Coffey, or George H. White. Use the library to find information.

4. Make a collage on African American involvement in the westward movement. Include copies of photos and drawings along with your own drawings of people and activities in this period. Use the library to find materials and information.

CHAPTER 10

ABOLITIONISTS: THE MORAL ATTACK ON ENSLAVEMENT
1800-1850

THE

UNDERGROUND RAIL ROAD.

A RECORD

OF

FACTS, AUTHENTIC NARRATIVES, LETTERS, &c.,

Narrating the Hardships Hair-breadth Escapes and Death Struggles

OF THE

Slaves in their efforts for Freedom,

AS RELATED

BY THEMSELVES AND OTHERS, OR WITNESSED BY THE AUTHOR;

TOGETHER WITH

SKETCHES OF SOME OF THE LARGEST STOCKHOLDERS, AND

MOST LIBERAL AIDERS AND ADVISERS,

OF THE ROAD.

BY

WILLIAM STILL,

For many years connected with the Anti-Slavery Office in Philadelphia, and Chairman
of the Acting Vigilant Committee of the Philadelphia Branch of
the Underground Rail Road.

Illustrated with 70 fine Engravings by Bensell, Schell and others, and
Portraits from Photographs from Life.

Thou shalt not deliver unto his master the servant that has escaped from his master unto thee.—*Deut.* xxiii. 16.

SOLD ONLY BY SUBSCRIPTION.

PHILADELPHIA:
PORTER & COATES,
822, CHESTNUT STREET.
1872.

 William Still wrote the most complete book of first-hand experiences about the Underground Railroad. He told of many violations of the Fugitive Slave Law of 1850. Afraid that he would be in danger, he hid his records in a church and graveyard.

This symbol comes from Congo, Kinshasa, and was created to look like a Bangba painted wall design.

Frederick Douglass was the most well-known African American abolitionist. But there were hundreds of others, both free and enslaved. In the early 1800s, they formed the ideas of the abolitionist movement.

In 1800, free African American men such as Absalom Jones and James Forten[1] went to Congress to speak against slavery. The first African American newspaper, *Freedom's Journal*, was printed in 1827. It spoke against slavery. David Walker published the first anti-slavery pamphlet in this country in 1829.

Richard Allen, with the help of forty free African American men, formed the first National Negro Convention in 1830 in Philadelphia. The men came from nine states. They met and worked to end slavery. The vice president of the convention was Austin Seward, a businessman from Rochester, New York. Other African American abolitionists were Henry Highland Garnet, Harriet Tubman, Richard Allen, Martin Delaney and Sojourner Truth. They worked against slavery in many ways. Some spoke for nonviolent protest. Others thought revolts were the best way to end the system of slavery. But they all knew one truth—that enslavement was against the principles of liberty on which the United States was founded.

Sometimes European Americans and African Americans worked together to end enslavement. For a while, Frederick Douglass worked with the Anti-Slavery Society, a group started by William Lloyd Garrison in 1831. The European Americans of the Anti-Slavery Society wished to end slavery, too. Douglass made speeches for them about the evils of enslavement. Often the white Americans thought they had the best ideas about how to do it. African Americans in these groups did not always agree with them. Sometimes they chose to form their own anti-slavery groups. The beliefs of the great men and women who fought enslavement were based on the principle of freedom for all. In 1839, David A. Payne said:

"I am opposed to slavery, not because it enslaves the black man, but because it enslaves man."

---

[1] *Absalom Jones* was the first Episcopalian priest in America of African descent. James Forten was a wealthy merchant. When the Anti-Slavery Society was running out of money, he gave them money to save it.

 Some enslaved people escaped to freedom with help from a network of abolitionists. The abolitionists included free African Americans and European Americans. The network was called the "underground railroad" because each "stop" was a safe house or place for those escaping. Enslaved people often had to travel at night so they were not caught before reaching free territory. The underground railroad helped several thousand, but most enslaved people who escaped had to make it on their own.

David Walker's Call for Action

The following first-person account is taken from *Eyewitness: The Negro in American History*, by William L. Katz, Pitman Publishers, 1964:

David Walker, born free in North Carolina, came to Boston where he learned to read and write. In his fiery pamphlet, written in 1829, he concluded that slave revolts were justified to end slavery and he advised Negroes to take action. He also had some words of advice for all Americans.

"...Remember, Americans, that we must and shall be free and enlightened as you are, will you wait until we shall, under God, obtain our liberty by the crushing arm of power? Will it not be dreadful for you? I speak Americans for your good. We must and shall be free I say, in spite of you. You may do your best to keep us in wretchedness and misery, to enrich you and your children, but God will deliver us from under you. And wo, wo will be to you if we have to obtain our freedom by fighting. Throw away your fears and prejudices then, and enlighten us and treat us like men, and we will like you more than we do now hate you, and tell us now no more about colonization to Africa, for America is much our country, as it is yours. Treat us like men, and there is no danger but we will all live in peace and happiness together. For we are not like you, hard hearted unmerciful, and unforgiving. What a happy country this will be, if the whites will listen. . . . But Americans, I declare to you, while you keep us and our children bondage, and treat us like brutes, to make us support you and your families, we cannot be your friends. You do not look for it, do you? Treat us then like men, and we will be your friends...."

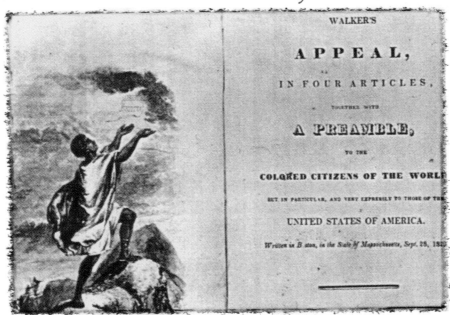

In 1829, David Walker printed his "Appeal" in the African American **Freedom's Journal**. This appeal was an angry attack on slavery.

 Harriet Tubman, at left, with family members and friends. In her fight as an abolitionist, she helped over 300 people escape from slavery.

Austin Seward was a pioneer of Rochester, New York, in the early 1800s. He was born in Virginia in 1793 and was enslaved until he was twenty-two years old. During the time of his enslavement, Seward was living in New York State with his "owner," Captain Helms. Austin Seward secretly talked to a lawyer about the slavery laws in New York. The lawyer told him that since Helms had hired him out to another farmer, he was, by law, free. Seward left Captain Helms and "took" his freedom.

In 1814, Seward worked for a farmer in the area and saved his wages. He moved to Rochester, New York, in 1817 and opened a meat market. His business was successful. Between 1817 and 1838, Austin Seward owned five businesses and several pieces of property. Seward had a general store in which he lived with his family. In addition to being a successful businessman, Seward was also a well-known abolitionist and orator (public speaker). He believed that all men should have equal rights and opportunities. He took part in many abolitionist meetings and traveled around the country speaking against slavery and injustice. In 1857, he wrote a book about his life called, *Twenty-Two Years a Slave and Forty Years a Freeman.*

 This poster of a slave asking to be treated as a brother was used widely by African Americans and antislavery whites to protest slavery.

ACTIVITY

CANAAN, NEW HAMPSHIRE AND NEGRO STUDENTS

The following first-person account is taken from *Eyewitness: The Negro in American History*, by William L. Katz, Pitman Publishers, 1964:

"[Negro students Alexander Crummel, Henry H. Garnet, and Thomas Sidney of New York were invited to attend school in Canaan, New Hampshire, in 1835. Alexander Crummell tells the story.]

It was a long and wearisome journey, of some four hundred and more miles; and rarely would an inn or a hotel give us food, and nowhere could we get shelter. . . The sight of three black youths, in gentlemanly garb, traveling through New England was, in those days, a most unusual sight; started not only surprise, but brought out universal sneers and ridicule. We met a most cordial reception at Canaan from two score white students, and began, with the highest hopes, our studies. But our stay was the briefest. . . . On the 4th of July, with wonderful taste and felicity, the farmers, from a wide region around, assembled at Canaan and resolved to remove the academy as a public nuisance. On the 10th of August they gathered together from the neighboring towns, seized the building, and with ninety yoke of oxen carried it off into a swamp about a half mile from its site. They were two days in accomplishing this miserable work. Meanwhile, under Garnet, as our leader, the boys in our boarding house were moulding bullets, expecting an attack upon our dwelling. About eleven o'clock at night the tramp of horses was heard approaching and as one rapid rider passed the house and fired at it, Garnet quickly replied by a discharge from a double-barreled shotgun which blazed away through the window. At once the hills, from many miles around, reverberated with the sound. Lights were seen in scores of houses on every side, and the towns and villages far and near were in a state of great excitement. But that musket shot by Garnet doubtless saved our lives. The cowardly ruffians dared not attack us..."

READING CRITICALLY AND WRITING

1. Write your own version of how these students felt and reacted. With a group, you may wish to turn your individual writings into a short play to perform for the class.

2. Research abolitionist Sojourner Truth's famous speech "Ain't I A Woman." Write a summary explaining what Truth was saying. In your opinion, was she a brave activist? Explain.

ACTIVITY

AFRICAN AMERICAN ABOLITIONISTS

HENRY HIGHLAND GARNET

SOJOURNER TRUTH

MARTIN DELANEY

JAMES FORTEN

RICHARD ALLEN

HARRIET TUBMAN

On a separate sheet of paper, write the names of the abolitionists shown on this page. Write an important piece of information about each abolitionist. Include the dates each abolitionist lived.

CHAPTER 10 REVIEW

Write your answers on a separate piece of paper.

VOCABULARY TO KNOW

Use context clues or a dictionary to help you write
definitions for the following words:

1. abolitionist
2. revolt

3. principle
4. convention

Thinking Critically

1. List some specific actions
   taken by African American
   abolitionists in the early
   1800s.

2. Explain the meaning of David A.
   Paynes's statement that
   appears on page 75.

3. Describe two different
   approaches that African
   American abolitionists took to
   end slavery.

Writing

4. Pretend you are an abolitionist.
   Write a speech against
   enslavement.

5. Explain the meaning of the
   following: "The African American
   abolitionist movement was
   based on a desire for all people
   to have liberty." How does this
   statement relate to David A.
   Payne's statement on page 75.

THE MISSOURI COMPROMISE & THE COMPROMISE OF 1850

1850

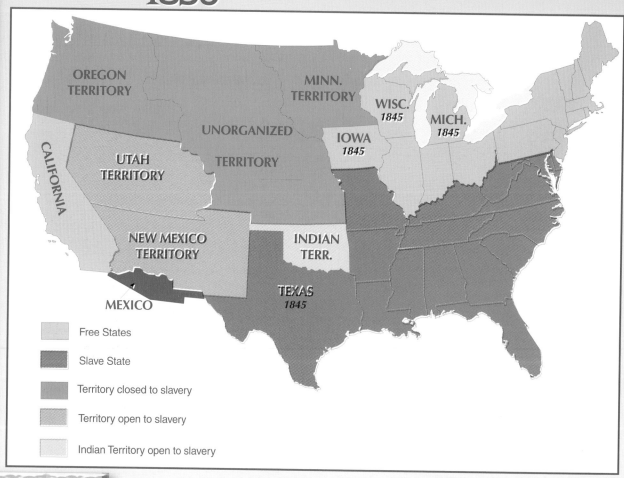

OREGON TERRITORY

MINN. TERRITORY

WISC. 1845

MICH. 1845

CALIFORNIA

UTAH TERRITORY

UNORGANIZED TERRITORY

IOWA 1845

NEW MEXICO TERRITORY

INDIAN TERR.

MEXICO

TEXAS 1845

Free States

Slave State

Territory closed to slavery

Territory open to slavery

Indian Territory open to slavery

The United States After the Missouri Compromise (1850)

This symbol comes from Ghana, and was created to look like an Ashanti bronze box design.

The Missouri Compromise and the Compromise of 1850 were made by leaders in the North and the South who were trying to settle disputes about slavery. Slavery existed in some states but not in others. During the early 1800s, the country was being divided into slave states and free states.

When people in an area of the country applied to be a state, Congress would argue about whether the new state should be slave or free. Both compromises, or "deals," were attempts to balance the number of free and slave states.

 Illustrations like this one showed slaves turning gratefully to the white man for their freedom. The artist's view of African Americans was that they depended only on the white man to give them their freedom. In this illustration, the artist shows a Union soldier reading the Emancipation Proclamation to happy slaves. In reality, the Emancipation Proclamation did not free slaves. It did not free slaves in states or towns taken by the Union army. It did not apply to states or towns that were not controlled by the Union army.

In neither compromise was the effect of enslavement on its victims considered. The Fugitive Slave Law was passed in 1850. At that time, California wanted to enter the Union as a free state. The South, in exchange, demanded the Fugitive Slave Law. It said that enslaved people who escaped should be sent back to their "owners" if they were caught anywhere in the country, even the free states.

African Americans worked hard to help enslaved people escape. The Fugitive Slave Law was fought by African American and white abolitionists. The Underground Railroad helped fewer people escape enslavement, but it became legendary as African Americans sought freedom. Thousands fled to freedom in Canada.

Enslaved people who freed themselves often helped other enslaved people escape. Reverend Jarmain Loguen was one of these men. In 1850, he lived in Syracuse, New York. His home and church were a stop on the underground railroad. He made a speech about the Fugitive Slave Law in which he said:

"... I don't respect this law—I don't fear it—I won't obey it! It outlaws me, and I outlaw it, and the men who attempt to enforce it on me. I place the government officials on the ground that they place me. I will not live a slave, and if force is employed to re-enslave me, I shall make preparations to meet the crisis as becomes a man."[1]

 Thomas Garrett (right), John Hunn (center) and Samuel Burris (left) led the Underground Railroad efforts in Delaware (a slave state). The Underground Railroad was made up of African Americans and European Americans alike.

1 *Eyewitness, The Negro in American History,* William L. Katz, 1964

 According to the Fugitive Slave Law, enslaved men and women could be taken from free states and forced to return to their "owners" in slave states. Here, a free woman and her child beg a rich Southerner not to take her husband.

ACTIVITY

REVEREND JARMAIN W. LOGUEN

The leaders who made laws and compromises about slavery did not see that a country that stood for freedom should not, at the same time, enslave anyone. They did not expect such a strong fight against these laws. The anti-slavery movement helped to push the country closer to war.

1. Memorize Reverend Jarmain Loguen's statement about the Fugitive Slave Law. Present the statement to the class. Be dramatic and convincing.

2. Write your own short speech to give about the Fugitive Slave Law. Remember that you must persuade with facts, but also sway people with your words. You want to move people to agree with you. Perform your speech for the class. (You may also do this activity as a group, with one member presenting.)

CHAPTER 11 REVIEW

Write your answers on a separate piece of paper.

VOCABULARY TO KNOW

Use context clues or a dictionary to help you write
definitions for the following words:

1. **Fugitive Slave Law**
2. **dispute**
3. **crisis**
4. **enforce**
5. **Emancipation Proclamation**

Thinking Critically

1. In your own words, tell who made the Missouri Compromise and the Compromise of 1850. Why were these compromises made?

2. Explain why the Missouri Compromise and the Compromise of 1850 did not work.

Writing

3. Pretend you are a newspaper editor in 1850. You believe that a country cannot be a democracy and have slavery at the same time. Write an article expressing your views on the Compromise of 1850.

4. Pretend you were alive in 1851. Write a letter to the editor of your local newspaper expressing your views about the Fugitive Slave Law.

AFRICANS, THE CIVIL WAR AND THE EMANCIPATION PROCLAMATION

1861-1865

 After the Emancipation Proclamation, African American men were actively recruited for the Union Army. About 200,000 African Americans joined the Northern armed forces after leaders like Frederick Douglass urged them to enlist.

This symbols comes from Ghana, and was created to look like the Ashanti "Adinkira" printed stamp.

About 200,000 African American men, both free and enslaved, fought in the Union army and navy during the Civil War. They fought in more than 400 battles and won many honors. Often they fought under racist officers. African Americans were given less training and poorer quality weapons than white soldiers. Still, their brave efforts helped the Union win many battles, and finally, the war.[1]

At the start of the war, African American men were not allowed to be soldiers. Why was this? How did it change? African Americans had fought in earlier wars such as the Revolutionary War. They tried to join the army to fight in this war too, but they were not allowed.

Thousands of slaves fled to the Union lines seeking freedom. They hoped the Union side would help them. But President Lincoln said no! He told his generals to return the slaves to their "owners." He said his purpose in fighting the war was to save the Union. It was not to end slavery. At that time, the border states of Delaware, Maryland, West Virginia, Kentucky and Missouri allowed slavery. Lincoln did not want these slave states to leave the Union and he thought that most whites in the North would not go to a war to end slavery.

When African American men were not allowed to fight in the Union forces, they helped in other ways. They gave aid and comfort to Union soldiers. They helped war prisoners who escaped. Some African American men and women were scouts and agents in the Union's spy system. Others worked in Union camps as laborers, nurses, cooks and mechanics.

Emancipation or Not?

Some men in Congress wanted to end slavery. They also wanted African American men to fight for the Union. The South was fighting hard and winning many battles. These leaders were no longer sure that the North could win the war. Some generals formed regiments of African American soldiers without waiting for orders. The soldiers fought well. This helped show Lincoln and the rest of Congress that larger numbers of African American soldiers could help to win the war. Lincoln told a member of his Cabinet that he had

"...come to the conclusion that it was a military necessity, absolutely necessary for the salvation of the nation, that we must free the slaves or be ourselves subdued"[2]

---

[1] African American soldiers won many major battles such as Port Hudson, Milliken's Bend and Fort Wagner. They also helped to win at Richmond, Petersburg and the Appomattox Court House..

[2] Diary of Gideon Welles, Gideon Welles, 1911, (Welles was the Secretary of the Navy under Lincoln).

In 1862, Congress made some decisions:

 ▼ In March, it forbade Union officers to return fugitive slaves to their "owners."

 ▼ In April, it passed a bill ending slavery in Washington, D.C.

 ▼ In July, it gave President Lincoln the power to take African American men as soldiers.

 ▼ In July it freed the slaves of all Confederate states, but left many African Americans in Union states still enslaved.

Later in July, Lincoln showed a draft of the Emancipation Proclamation to his Cabinet. They thought the time was not right to issue the proclamation. They said he should wait to issue it after a big battle was won. They did not want it to look as if the Union was weak or that the Union was in need of African American men to help win the war. In the meeting, Secretary of State William H. Seward said: " . . . It may be viewed as the last measure of an exhausted government, a cry for help." [3]

Lincoln listened to his Cabinet and waited. In September 1862, the Union won the battle of Antietam. Lincoln warned the South that he would free all slaves in the Confederate states on January 1, 1863. On that day he put forth the Emancipation Proclamation. It did not give freedom to all African Americans who were enslaved. Slaves in the border states were not freed until the 13th Amendment was passed in 1865. But now the Union could recruit large numbers of African Americans to be soldiers. It could get the help it needed to win the war.

President Abraham Lincoln delivered the Emancipation Proclamation in September of 1862. The Proclamation freed slaves in the Confederate states on January 1, 1863. However, slaves on the border of the North and the South were not free until the 13th Amendment was passed two years later.

3 *Before the Mayflower*, Lerone Bennett, Jr. 1982.

African American soldiers are shown above returning to their families after the Civil War ended.

The following first-person account is taken from *Eyewitness: The Negro in American History*, by William L. Katz, Pitman Publishers, 1964:

In the months following the end of the Civil War, Negroes met in the Southern states to formulate their plans and desires as free men. The group that met at the First Baptist Church of Norfolk, Virginia, on December 1865, drew up these resolutions.

"We are a peaceable and law abiding people and that the stories so industriously circulated against us that we are contemplating and preparing for insurrection and riotous and disorderly proceedings are vile falsehoods designed to provoke acts of unlawful violence against us. . . . We have faith in God and our country and in the justice and humanity of the American people for redress of all our grievances but that we will not cease to importune and labor in all lawful and proper ways for equal rights as citizens until finally granted. . . . We appoint [a committee] to proceed to Washington to urge upon Congress such legislation as will secure, to the lately rebellious states, a republican form of Government and the consequent protection to ourselves of life, liberty, and property and of the granting of our people in those states of the right to testify in the courts and of equality of suffrage the same as to white citizens. That said committee be empowered to represent us before the Freedmen's Bureau at Washington. . . to secure, if possible, the selection and nomination . . . of the local agents by the Freedmen themselves. . ."

ACTIVITY

EMANCIPATION PROCLAMATION—1862

Whereas, on the twenty-second day of September, in the year of our Lord one thousand eight hundred and sixty-two, a proclamation was issued by the President of the United States, containing, among other things, the following, to wit::

That on the first day of January, in the year of our Lord one thousand eight hundred and sixty-three, all persons held as slaves within any State, or designated part of a State, the people whereof shall then be in rebellion against the United States, shall be then, thenceforward, and forever free; and the Executive Government of the United States, including the military and naval authority thereof, will do no acts to retain the freedom of such persons, and will do no act or acts to repress such persons, or any of them, in any efforts they may make for their actual freedom.

That the Executive will, on the first day of January aforesaid, by proclamation, designate the States and parts of States, if any, in which the people thereof respectively shall then be in rebellion against the United States; and the fact that any State, or the people thereof, shall on that day be in good faith represented in the Congress of the United States by members chosen thereto at elections wherein a majority of the qualified voters of such State shall have participated, shall in the absence of strong countervailing testimony be deemed conclusive evidence that such State and the people thereof are not then in rebellion against the United States.

Now, therefore, I, Abraham Lincoln, President of the United States, by virtue of the power in me vested as Commander-in-Chief of the Army and Navy of the United States, in time of actual armed rebellion against the authority and government of the United States, and as a fit and necessary war measure for suppressing said rebellion, do on this first day of January, in the year of our Lord one thousand eight hundred and sixty-three, and in accordance with my purpose so to do, publicly proclaimed for the full period of 100 days from the day first above mentioned, order and designate as the States and parts of states wherein the people thereof, respectively, are this day in rebellion against the United States, the following to wit: Arkansas, Texas, Louisiana (except the parishes of St. Bernard, Plaquemines, Jefferson, St. John, St. Charles,

St. James, Ascension, Assumption, Terre Bonne, Lafourche, St. Mary, Martin, and Orleans, including the city of New Orleans), Mississippi, Alabama, Florida, Georgia, South Carolina, North Carolina, and Virginia (except the forty-eight counties designated as West Virginia, and also the counties of Berkeley, Accomac, Northampton, Elizabeth City, York, Princess Anne, and Norfolk, including the cities of Norfolk and Portsmouth), and which excepted parts are for the present left precisely as if this proclamation were not issued.

And by virtue of the power and for the purpose aforesaid, I do order and declare that all persons held as slaves within said designated States and parts of States are, and henceforward shall be, free; and that the Executive Government of the United States, including the military and naval authorities thereof, shall recognize and maintain the freedom of said persons. And I hereby enjoin upon the people so declared to be free to abstain from all violence, unless in necessary self-defense; and I recommend to them that, in all cases where allowed, they labor faithfully for reasonable wages.

And I further declare and make known that such persons of suitable condition will be received into the armed service of the United States to garrison forts, positions, stations, and other places, and man vessels of all sorts in said service.

And upon this act, sincerely believed to be an act of justice, warranted by the Constitution upon military necessity, I invoke the considerate judgment of mankind and the gracious favor of Almighty God.

In witness whereof, I have hereunto set my hand and caused the seal of the United States to be affixed. Done at the city of Washington, the first day of January, in the year of our Lord one thousand eight hundred and sixty-three, and of the independence of the United States of America the eighty-seventh.

By the President
Abraham Lincoln

William H. Seward, Secretary of State

1. Write your own summary of the Emancipation Proclamation. Explain what each paragraph means.

2. Write your own opinion of Lincoln's Emancipation Proclamation. Was it leading the country in a good direction or not? Explain your thinking.

CHAPTER 12 REVIEW

Write your answers on a separate piece of paper.

VOCABULARY TO KNOW

Use context clues or a dictionary to help you write definitions for the following words:

1. issue
2. subdue
3. salvation
4. conclusion
5. forbade
6. recruit
7. Cabinet

Thinking Critically

1. Describe the different types of African involvement in the Civil War.

2. Describe the events which led to the issuing of the Emancipation Proclamation.

3. Explain why African American soldiers were needed to win the Civil War.

Writing

4. Write a paragraph titled: "Why Lincoln Issued the Emancipation Proclamation." Use the actual document and any other references you find for reasons to support your paragraph.

5. Imagine that you are an African American who wants to enlist in the Union army. Write a letter to President Lincoln explaining why you think the policy that does not allow African Americans to fight in the war should be changed. Give examples of how you and your friends have already helped the Union side.

6. Use a map of the United States to locate the border states of Delaware, Maryland, West Virginia, Kentucky, and Missouri. Did the Emancipation Proclamation end slavery in these states in 1862? If the Emancipation Proclamation did not end all slavery in America, why do you think it was written? Explain.

CHAPTER 13

INNOVATIONS AND INVENTIONS OF A FREE PEOPLE

1700s–1900s

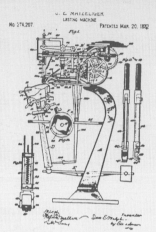

J. E. Matzelinger's model for a shoe lasting machine brought about the mass production of shoes. He patented this model.

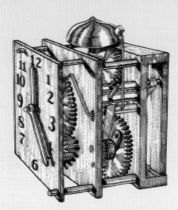

Benjamin Bannaker built the first all-wood clock in America. He carved the entire clock by hand, including the running parts inside.

George Washington Carver created more than 200 uses for peanuts. Dr. Carver also taught farmers that legume plants such as peanuts take nitrogen from the air and give it out through their roots. This helps enrich the soil so the farmers can plant other crops.

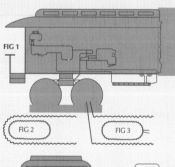

Granville Woods's Railway Induction Telegraph System helped to eliminate many train collisions. This is a diagram of it.

This symbol comes from Bida, Nigeria, and was created to look like a mud wall design.

Benjamin Bannaker was born in Maryland, November 9, 1731, of a mother who was free and a father who was enslaved. Fortunately, Benjamin Bannaker was never enslaved. Bannaker learned to read at an early age and spent all of his spare time studying science and mathematics. He became a close friend of George Ellicott, a member of a Quaker family. Their friendship was based on their common interest in mathematics and the natural sciences. Ellicott lent Bannaker books and instruments. The knowledge gained from these books led Bannaker to a lifelong study of astronomy. Bannaker made the first wooden striking clock with all American parts. Although he had never seen one, he was able to construct the clock with the only tool he had, a pocket knife. Bannaker also published one of the first series of almanacs in the United States. The highest honor given to Bannaker was to be asked to serve on the commission that surveyed and planned the city of Washington, D.C. When the head of the commission left to live in France without finishing the plans for the city, Benjamin Bannaker completed the task from memory. Bannaker became the main force in planning the city of Washington, D.C. He died in 1806.

Jan Ernst Matzeliger was born in Dutch Guiana in 1852. He died of

Inventor Benjamin Bannaker served on a planning commission for the contruction of the city of Washington, D.C.

tuberculosis in 1889. In his short life, he became famous for his mechanical genius. Matzeliger moved to Lynn, Massachusetts, in 1876.

While working in shoe factories in Lynn and Boston, he began to experiment with shoe-lasting by machines. Matzeliger continued to work on his own ideas for ten years. His first machine was made of wood. A later model was made of scrap iron. Finally, he applied to Washington, D.C. for a patent for his invention.

◆ Jan Ernst Matzeliger

make his way alone in the world. He studied much on his own and worked his way through Simpson College and Iowa State College.

Dr. Carver, a research scientist, taught at Tuskegee Institute. He educated farmers in the ways of getting more crops from the soil. He made hundreds of discoveries during his lifetime. Some of his products were served in the cafeteria of Tuskegee Institute. Many of his discoveries were used by private industry.

Dr. Carver made more than two hundred different products from the peanut and more than one hundred

Matzeliger's diagrams were too complex for the patent reviewers to understand. An agent came from Washington to see the model shoe-lasting machine, and on March 20, 1883, Jan E. Matzeliger was granted patent N274,207. His invention allowed the shoemaker to shape the upper leather over the last (shoe form) and attach this leather to the bottom part of the shoe. Because the process could be done rapidly with the aid of this machine, Matzeliger's invention was worth millions of dollars to the shoe industry.

George Washington Carver was born in 1864 in Diamond Grove, Missouri. At the age of thirteen, he was forced to

◆ Dr. George Washington Carver

different products from the sweet potato. From the soybean, he obtained flour, breakfast food, and milk. He found more than five hundred shades of dye to replace aniline dyes imported from Germany. His work on dehydration was of interest to the United States government, and he was called to Washington to report on his findings.

Dr. Carver's main work, in addition to his research, was to show the use of science and scientific techniques to improve the land. It is felt that Dr. Carver did more for southern farming at the time, and perhaps ever, than any other person. Because of his findings, the South did not depend only on cotton as its chief crop. The peanut and the sweet potato became major crops in the South.

Granville T. Woods

Granville T. Woods was born in Columbus, Ohio, on April 23, 1856. He attended school until the age of ten. Working and going to college helped him to get a mechanical and engineering background. Granville T. Woods invented many things. He started his own company which sold his telegraph and his other inventions. On April 1, 1887, the Catholic Tribune described him as "the greatest electrician in the world." The greatest of his inventions was the induction telegraph. This was a system of communication to and from moving trains. It prevented railroad accidents by keeping each train informed of the locations of other nearby trains.

Many of Mr. Woods' inventions were sold to the American Bell Telephone Company and the General Electric Company. He sold his air brake patent to the Westinghouse Air Brake Company. Mr. Woods was granted more than thirty-five patents. He and other African American inventors played a large role in improving the railroads in the United States. Transporting goods and people by railroad was very important to the development of American industry. Granville T. Woods died in 1910.

These are only a small number of African American innovaters and inventors who worked for better life while continuing to fight racism. Many books have been written about these African American men and women who soared ahead as they left slavery behind. You will want to read more about them on your own.

Lewis Howard Latimer was born in Boston in 1848. He served as a sailor in the Civil War. After the war, he learned drafting and electrical engineering and became a draft person. In 1876, he met Alexander Graham Bell and began to work with him. Latimer made drawings for Bell's telephone patents.

A few years later, he invented an incandescent electric light with Hiram S. Maxim. In 1844, he joined the staff of Thomas Edison and became one of the famous Edison Pioneers. He wrote a book explaining the use and workings of the electric light.

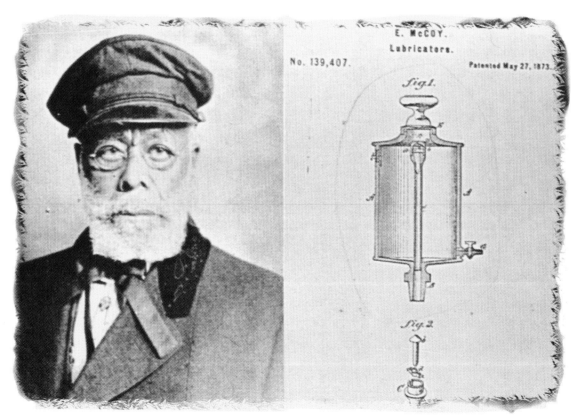

Elijah McCoy invented a lubricating cup in 1872 that fed oil to parts of a machine while it was running. This was so helpful in operating trains and factory machines that people would ask for the "real McCoy" for their machines. This is where the expression "the real McCoy" comes from.

The following first-person account is taken from *Eyewitness: The Negro in American History*, by William L. Katz, Pitman Publishers, 1964:

[George H. Murray, a former slave who was an orphan by Emancipation time, managed to educate himself and spent two years at South Carolina University, until all Negroes were expelled in 1876. In 1892 he was elected to the United States Congress where he championed the causes of free silver and Negro education. On August 10, 1894 he told his white colleagues in the House of Representatives of Negro progress, even in the difficult field of invention.]

We have proven in almost every line that we are capable of doing what other people can do. We have proven that we can work as much and as well as other people. We have proven that we can learn as well as other people. We have proven that we can fight as well as other people, as was demonstrated in the late [Civil] war. There are still, however, traducers and slanderers of our race who claim that we are not equal to others because we have failed to produce inventors....

I hold in my hand a statement prepared by one of the assistants in the Patent Office, showing the inventions that have been made by colored men within the past few years. . .

This statement shows that colored men have taken out patents on almost everything, from a cooking stove to a locomotive. Patents have been granted to colored men for inventions and improvements in the workshop, on the farm, in the factory, on the railroad, in the mine, in almost every department of labor, and some of the most important improvements that go to make up that great motive power of modern industrial machinery, the steam engine, have been produced by colored men.

. . .Mr. Speaker, the colored people of this country want an opportunity to show that the progress, that the civilization which is now admired the world over, that the civilization which is now leading the world, that the civilization which all the nations of the world look up to and imitate—the colored people, I say, want an opportunity to show that they, too, are part and parcel of that great civilization. Mr. Speaker, in conclusion I ask the liberty [of] appending to my remarks the statistics to which I referred.

There was no objection.

Congressman Murray then submitted the list of 92 patents. Eight of them were patents which he held.

ACTIVITY

Below is a list of more African American inventors. Read what each contributed to America. Write a biography about the person of your choice.

MORE AFRICAN AMERICAN INVENTORS

NAME	DATE OF BIRTH	OCCUPATION	CONTRIBUTION
Elijah McCoy	middle 1800s	Inventor	Lubricating cup for machines in operation.
Lewis Howard Latimer	1848	Draftsman	Invented a method of making carbon filaments which made the Maixim Light Bulb the first long-burning bulb.
Norbert Rillieux	1806	Instructor of Applied Mechanics at a school in Paris	Invented the triple effect evaporator used in sugar refining (a vacuum pan).
Dr. Charles Drew	1904	Surgeon	Developed method for storing blood, plasma and modern blood-bank system (1940).
Madame C.J. Walker	1867	Inventor/ Business woman	Invented many chemical preparations and aids for treatment of hair and skin.
Dr. Percy Lanon Julian	1899	Chemist	Synthesized drug for treatment of glaucoma, 1935.
Dr. William Hinton	1833	Hematologist	Developed test for syphilis.
Garret Morgan	1875	Inventor	Invented gas inhalator and automatic stop sign for automobiles.
Dr. Daniel Hale Williams	1856	Physician and Surgeon	First surgeon to operate on the human heart.
James Forten	1766	Merchant	Invented a method of sewing large, heavy sails for big ships.
Henry Blair	early 1800s	Inventor	Corn-planting machine.

CHAPTER 13 REVIEW

Write your answers on a separate piece of paper.

VOCABULARY TO KNOW

Use context clues or a dictionary to help you write
definitions for the following words:

1. **invention**
2. **astronomy**
3. **dehydration**
4. **complex**
5. **engineering**
6. **almanac**

Thinking Critically

1. Make a chart of African American scientists and inventors and their achievements for your classroom. Use information from your school library.

2. Explain how inventions have improved the quality of life in the U.S.

Writing

3. Pretend you are one of the inventors from the "More African American Inventors" chart on page 100. Write a letter to a friend, describing your work. Include details from your daily life. Tell what you like best about your work and describe one or two of the problems you have had. Use the library for facts and details to include in your letter.

4. Do research, either by yourself or with a group. Add at least three African American inventors to the chart on page 100, or make your own new chart.

CHAPTER 14

THE FIRST RECONSTRUCTION

1867-1877

This symbol comes from the Lower Congo and was created to look like a carving on a wooden keg.

 In Washington D.C. in 1867, African American men voted with European American men for the first time. The clerks who registered the votes were also both African and European Americans. This caused tension and rioting in many parts of the country.

The period between 1867 and 1877 was known as Reconstruction. It was an important time in history. The Civil War was over. Now the country had to be put back together. What did this mean for African Americans?

President Lincoln did not have a plan to help freedmen when the Civil War ended. When Andrew Johnson became President after Lincoln's death, he did not have a plan for helping freedmen, either. Most freedmen had no jobs and did not own a place to live or grow food. Poor whites had problems, too. Both groups needed food, clothing and shelter. They also needed jobs, education and land. The Freedmen's Bureau was created in 1865 to provide for these needs.

African American leaders such as Frederick Douglass knew that these needs must be met. A few white leaders such as Thaddeus Stevens also knew this. They wanted the South to rebuild. They wanted African Americans to take an equal part in this rebirth. Laws were made by Congress at this time to protect all Americans.

President Andrew Johnson began to pardon Southern landowners who had been part of the Confederacy. He gave them back their lands. He made white men governors of states in the South. All-white governments were formed. It was no surprise that African Americans were not helped by the new Southern leaders.

These all-white Southern governments passed laws called "black codes" to take rights away from free men. Hundreds of African Americans were arrested, beaten and put in jail even though they had committed no crimes. Others were forced to work on the plantations of their former masters. People who resisted were beaten or murdered.

Many leaders in Congress became angry. They took control of Reconstruction away from President Johnson. Congress passed laws that put the South under martial law, or the control of the army. Now freedmen were given the right to vote. They were protected by troops from the North when they went to the polls. In some states, there were more African American voters than white voters. At times, African Americans were able to elect their own African American leaders.

Not all whites in the South opposed African Americans. African American and white leaders in many states in the South worked with each other. They wrote laws. They tried to make democracy work for everyone. During this time, African American men served in the Congress and in state senates. They held other positions such as judges, school superintendents, mayors and police officers, too.

Disguised members of groups such as the Ku Klux Klan terrorized and murdered African Americans. They were responsible for hanging, burning, beating and murdering countless innocent people. Often, they killed entire families of African Americans in their homes.

Reconstruction Helps a Little

During Reconstruction, Congress passed the Civil Rights Bill of 1875. Congress also passed the 14th and 15th Amendments and added them to the Constitution.[1] These laws said that all people could vote and should be treated the same in public places.

Many whites in the South reacted with violence to the new laws. Some joined secretive and violent groups to punish African Americans and others who supported African American rights. The Ku Klux Klan (KKK) and other groups threatened, harmed, and sometimes murdered innocent African Americans. Many African Americans died at the hands of the KKK and similar groups. In many places, special rules and laws were made so that African Americans could not vote. African Americans who tried to vote were often killed. This violence began to destroy the gains that had been made with the Civil War and Reconstruction. New members of Congress did not want to keep the laws and policies that were brought about during the Reconstruction period.

◆ European American school teachers who believed in and taught equality were often threatened by the Ku Klux Klan.

1 The 14th and 15th Amendments are shown in more detail in Chapter 15.

Reconstruction came to an end when the North said it would pull its troops out of the South.[2] There was now "home rule" in the South. This meant that African American people in the South lost the military protection of the U.S. government. Local white leaders were now in control. They could once again treat African Americans unequally and unfairly.

The Reconstruction period was short-lived, but it was very important. It was a time when African Americans and white Americans worked with each other. They worked for equality. They tried to make the Constitution and the Declaration of Independence work for all Americans. The dream did not die.

During Reconstruction, many Americans of both African and European descent worked together toward equality.

[2] See Chapter 16, Compromise of 1877, page 116.

Reverend Henry M. Turner

During Reconstruction, Reverend Henry M. Turner was elected to the Georgia State Legislature, but white legislators would not allow him to take his seat. When this happened, Reverend Turner said to them "I am here to demand my rights, and to hurl thunderbolts at the men who would dare to cross the threshold of my manhood." But the Georgia Legislature refused to seat him and several other African American legislators.

On November 3, 1868, John W. Menard ran for Congress from the state of Louisiana. He defeated his white opponent with a vote of 5,107 to 2,833. He was the first African American elected to Congress. On December 21, 1868, some Congressmen congratulated him, but his opponent questioned his election. On February 27, Congress decided not to admit him. Congressman James A. Garfield said: "it was too early to admit a Negro to the U.S. Congress." Menard spoke in his own defense, becoming the first African American to make a speech in Congress.

 John W. Menard defeated his European American opponent by more than two thousand votes.

ACTIVITY

RECONSTRUCTION

Fill in the missing words or phrases on separate paper.

1. Reconstruction occurred between ____ and ____ .

2. Poor whites and African Americans needed ____ , ____ , ____ and ____ after the Civil War.

3. The black codes were a way to bring back ____ in another form.

4. After the war, African American and white leaders wrote laws that tried to make democracy work for ____ .

5. During Reconstruction, African American men served in Congress and State Senates. They also were ____ , ____ , ____ and ____ .

6. Congress passed the 14th Amendment in 1868, the 15th Amendment in 1870, and the Civil Rights Bill in 1875. These laws said ____ .

7. During Reconstruction, African American men were sometimes killed when they went to the polls to ____ .

8. "Home rule" meant that African American people in the South lost the ____ of the United States Government.

9. Reconstruction was a time when white and African American men worked with each other. They worked for ____ and to ____ .

10. "____ , ____ ," passed by Southern governments, took away the rights of African Americans.

ACTIVITY

Joseph Hayne Rainey was the first black elected to the U.S. House of Representatives.

Blanche K. Bruce served as Senator of Louisiana from 1875 to 1881.

The words below are found in Chapter 14. Using context clues and a dictionary, find the meaning of each word. Be sure to select the meaning that best fits the definition in this chapter. On a separate sheet of paper, write each word and its meaning. Then write a sentence in which you correctly use each word.

1. Reconstruction
2. amendment
3. black codes
4. rebirth
5. Americans
6. democracy
7. constitution
8. reconstruct

9. polls
10. governor
11. majority
12. innocent
13. congress
14. violence
15. superintendent
16. freedmen

17. Now write your own explanation of Reconstruction using all of the words above. Underline each word when you use it.

ACTIVITY

AFRICAN AMERICAN MEMBERS OF CONGRESS DURING RECONSTUCTION

Use the school or public library to find information about one of the members of Congress pictured below. Write a short biography about the person you choose.

RESEARCHING AND WRITING

The picture above shows seven of the fourteen African American Congressmen who served during Reconstruction. (Top Row) Robert C. DeLarge, Jefferson H. Long (Front Row) Hiram R. Revels, Benjamin S. Turner, Josiah T. Walls, Joseph H. Rainy, R. Brown Elliot.

CHAPTER 14 REVIEW

Write your answers on a separate piece of paper.

VOCABULARY TO KNOW

Use context clues or a dictionary to help you write definitions for the following words:

1. amendment
2. democracy
3. short-lived
4. Reconstruction

Thinking Critically

1. Why did Congress take control of Reconstruction away from President Johnson and put the South under military control?

2. List some of the government positions held by African Americans during Reconstruction.

Writing

3. Write an essay titled "The Importance of Reconstruction in American History."

4. Make a poster with scenes of the important gains and struggles of the Reconstruction period. Illustrate your poster. Each scene should be titled and have a brief description.

15

THADDEUS STEVENS AND CHARLES SUMNER: POLITICS AND ETHICS

1860-1875

 Congressman
Thaddeus Stevens

Congressman
Charles Sumner

Stevens and Sumner worked together to make the anti-slavery beliefs of many African Americans and European Americans part of U.S. law. Like many, they believed the Declaration of Independence and Constitution was for all men.

This symbol originated in Northern Nigeria and was created to look like the pattern woven onto cloth.

For more than two hundred years, millions of African Americans were enslaved in this land. Many people opposed a legal system of slavery. African American people, enslaved or free, opposed it. Some European people were against slavery, too. They too wanted to abolish slavery. Why should anyone have the right to take away another person's freedom?

There are many ways to make one's beliefs known. Some people talk about their beliefs, but they don't do anything to put their beliefs into action. Other people will give up time and energy to fight for their beliefs. Some people even give up their lives for their beliefs.

In the 1800s, there were not many European Americans who opposed slavery in any effective or active way. Those who did worked to end slavery with African American abolitionists. They wanted to change laws which deprived millions of African Americans of their freedom. Thaddeus Stevens and Charles Sumner were two of these men. Before the Civil War, they worked to end slavery. After the war, they worked to protect African Americans and their rights. They believed that all Americans had equal rights.

Thaddeus Stevens and Charles Sumner were Congressmen. After the Civil War, they convinced Congress to do many things. Congress set up Reconstruction governments in the South. It passed laws, such as the Civil Rights Bill of 1875, to protect African Americans. Congress created the Freedmen's Bureau and sent soldiers to the South to make sure that African American men could vote. Congress also passed the 14th and 15th Amendments to the Constitution.

Stevens and Sumner wanted freedmen to be given land (40 acres each) of their own. The land would prevent the freedmen from having to depend on their former "masters" for a place to live and work. Congress would not pass such a law. Charles Sumner pushed for a Civil Rights Bill. The bill was to ban discrimination and segregation in most public places. The bill was passed in 1875 the year after Charles Sumner died.

Thaddeus Stevens and Charles Sumner shared a very deep belief in the Declaration of Independence and in the Constitution. They knew that freedom and liberty would be no more than words if these ideas did not apply to all Americans.

ACTIVITY

Read the summaries of the 14th and 15th Amendments below. Imagine that the year is 1875. Write a speech explaining why each amendment should be passed.

The Fourteenth Amendment to the U.S. Constitution 1868

The Constitution says that no state will make or enforce any law which limits the privileges of citizens of the United States; no state will deprive any person of life, liberty or property without due process of law; a state must not deny to any person within its jurisdiction the equal protection of the laws.

The Fifteenth Amendment to the U.S. Constitution 1870

The Constitution says that the rights of the citizens of the United States to vote will not be denied or limited by the United States or by any state because of a person's race color or previous condition of servitude.

CHAPTER 15 REVIEW

Write your answers on a separate piece of paper.

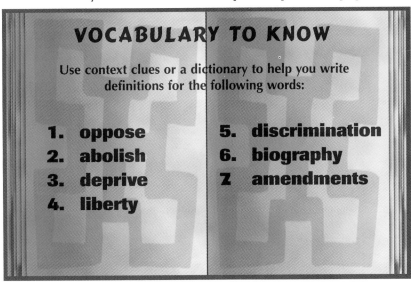

VOCABULARY TO KNOW

Use context clues or a dictionary to help you write definitions for the following words:

1. oppose
2. abolish
3. deprive
4. liberty

5. discrimination
6. biography
7. amendments

Thinking Critically

1. List some of the changes Thaddeus Stevens and Charles Sumner convinced Congress to make after the Civil War.

2. Identify one thing that Charles Sumner and Thaddeus Stevens worked to accomplish but could not.

Writing

3. Read the ideas of the 14th and 15th Amendments on page 114. In a paragraph, explain why Thaddeus Stevens and Charles Sumner wanted these amendments added to the Constitution.

4. Write a biography of Thaddeus Stevens or Charles Sumner. Use library references.

5. Do leaders today act on their beliefs? Write your own essay, individually or as a group, about a leader who acted on his or her beliefs to end inequality.

THE COMPROMISE OF 1877: THE END OF RECONSTRUCTION

1877

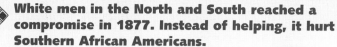

White men in the North and South reached a compromise in 1877. Instead of helping, it hurt Southern African Americans.

This symbol originated in Cameroon and was created to look like a beadwork design on a Bali Calabash cover.

The Compromise of 1877 was an agreement between white men in both the North and the South. It did not help African people in the South. It harmed them even more.

In 1877, there were many problems between the North and the South. The South was still under military rule. Southern landowners were angry about this. Leaders in both places were tired of dealing with the problems that resulted from the Civil War and the system of slavery. They wanted to get on with developing businesses from which they could profit.

Leaders in the North and the South reached a compromise. White Northern Republicans and white Southern Democrats agreed on the following:

Rutherford Hayes, a Republican from the North would be President of the United States.

The Southern landowners would have picked a Democrat, but agreed to Hayes because he did not support equal rights for African American people.

The U.S. Army would leave the South.

African Americans living in the South would have no military protection.

The South would have "home rule."

Local leaders in the South could now treat African Americans as they wished. No one from the North would stop them.

 By the end of the Reconstruction, African Americans in the South had made no progress towards freedom. Southern governments did not have to obey the laws of the North. President Lincoln's promises did not apply to Southern African Americans at all.

The Compromise of 1877 helped white groups who were in power in both the North and the South. Men who had been enemies during the Civil War were now friends. Without troops from the North, Southern leaders could take away rights from African Americans. One way they did this was by taking away the vote of African Americans through threats, attacks, poll taxes, hiding the polling places, literacy tests and even murder. Without the vote, African Americans could not elect leaders who would fight for laws to protect them. Without these laws, white landowners could continue to take advantage of African American workers.

African Americans were paid very low wages, lower than whites were paid. They had to pay for the land they rented by giving most of their crops back to the landowner. This was called sharecropping. European landowners made a lot of money from the sharecropping system. They were able to sell their products to Northern factory owners for low prices and still make a profit

The Northern factory owners profited, too. For example, owners of clothing factories in the North bought cotton at low prices from Southern landowners. They made clothes and sold them at a large profit. Leaders and merchants in both the South and the North gained from the Compromise of 1877, but equality and freedom were pushed farther out of reach. Most of the gains of Reconstruction were lost. African Americans became the working poor.

After the Civil War, most ex-slaves remained in the South. They had no land of their own and no money. They had to keep working on the plantations as sharecroppers.

This struggle over the Speaker's chair in the Louisiana state house, January 4, 1875, shows the resistance of European Americans to share their voting power with African Americans.

ACTIVITY

1. By yourself or in a small group, write both sides of an argument between a Northerner and a Southerner over military rule and slavery. Prepare your arguments as a debate to be performed for the class. Be accurate historically.

2. Pretend you are an African leader watching the Compromise of 1877 from your own African country. Your country is free and not a colony. Write a letter to President Hayes to explain how you view the situation as a non-African American.

Write your answers on a separate piece of paper.

VOCABULARY TO KNOW

Use context clues or a dictionary to help you write definitions for the following words:

1. **sharecropping**
2. **agreement**
3. **military rule**
4. **literacy**
5. **equal rights**
6. **polling**

Thinking Critically

1. Explain how the Compromise of 1877 caused many of the gains of Reconstruction to be lost.

2. Explain how Southern landowners and Northern factory owners benefited from the Compromise of 1877.

3. Explain how the end of the Reconstruction may have temporarily hurt African Americans. Discuss sharecropping in your explanation.

Writing

4. Write a short story about a Northern white factory owner and a Southern white landowner making a business deal in the year 1879. How might the Compromise of 1877 help each of these people?

5. Most African Americans in the South lost the right to vote as a result of the Compromise of 1877. Write a paragraph explaining how losing the vote affected these Americans.

THE ERA OF LEGAL SEGREGATION AND THE KU KLUX KLAN

1868-1900

 Ku Klux Klan Parade in Washington

This symbol originated in Ghana, and was created to look like an Ashanti "Adinkira" printing stamp pattern.

After the Civil War, laws such as the 13th, 14th and 15th Amendments were passed by Congress. These laws ended enslavement and guaranteed full rights to all Americans. The new laws stated that being a "slave" in the past was not a reason to deny a person the rights that other Americans enjoyed.

Many European Americans refused to accept these new laws. They continued to ignore the rights of African Americans. Former slave owners, who now made large profits from sharecropping, did not want to give up control of African American workers. Others feared competition for jobs. Some elected leaders feared losing their positions. Many European Americans feared that their way of life would change.

By the end of Reconstruction, the 1877 "home rule" was in place in the South.[1] This allowed Southern white leaders to treat African Americans as they wished. Government and business leaders of the South developed many ways to segregate, or keep African Americans and European Americans apart. The purpose of segregation was to bring back a way of life similar to slavery. The Reconstruction period had taught these white leaders a lesson—that they had less political power when African Americans and European Americans worked together.

Freedom Fades with Jim Crow

In order to gain back their power and wealth, Southern landowners began spreading lies about African Americans. Poor ignorant whites were told that African Americans had caused all their poverty. Leaders also made laws, called Jim Crow Laws, which did not allow African Americans and white people to use the same public places or to play or live together. At times, white Americans and African Americans worked together, but not on an equal basis or with the same pay for the same work.

African Americans were treated unfairly by judges and juries in many courts in the country. In many places, an African American could not testify against a white person. White people could commit crimes against African Americans and not be punished.

Lynch mobs abused the Jim Crow laws. The lynch mobs often attacked, hung, mutilated or burned innocent African Americans. Between 1882 and 1900, about 1,617 African Americans were lynched in this country.[2]

---

[1] For an explanation of "home rule," see Chapter 14 on Reconstruction

[2] *Before the Mayflower*, Lerone Bennett, Jr., 1982

This type of violence and brutality was used to oppress and keep African Americans apart from white people. People who tried to oppose the system of segregation were punished or killed. Through fear and violence, many people embraced racism or became silent and submissive.

African American Leaders Succeed

Many great African Americans worked for their people during these times. Ida B. Wells Barnett was a great journalist who stood up against lynching. Her life was threatened more than once as she wrote and spoke about the brutality of the lynchings of African American men. Booker T. Washington started a school named Tuskegee Institute for African Americans. He felt that basic education[3] and hard work were the ways for African Americans to make progress. Washington said that the races could be "apart" socially, but could work closely in areas which would help both groups, such as business.

Some wealthy European Americans gave money to help Booker T. Washington and his school. They liked Washington's ideas because they could be used to support segregation.

Dr. W.E.B. DuBois was another African American thinker and leader. He spoke about full equal rights in all areas of life. He and many others worked for this.[4] They opposed segregation. They also felt that hard work and education were ways to get ahead. DuBois wanted African American students to have an equal chance for a college education.

 W.E.B. DuBois

[3] This means a technical education in the trades with jobs such as masons, carpenters, farmers and plumbers.

[4] Others were Ida B. Wells, P.B.S. Pinchback, Dr. Daniel Hale Williams and Mary McLeod Bethune

Ida B. Wells Barnett

 Booker T. Washington

 Booker T. Washington started Tuskegee University as a college for African Americans. Some European Americans supported Washington and his ideas because they supported segregation.

Plessy v. Ferguson

In 1896, African American Homer Plessy was arrested for taking a seat on a "white" train. In the historical Supreme Court case of Plessy v. Ferguson, the Supreme Court ruled that Plessy was wrong. The court said that laws which kept African Americans and European Americans apart did not take away the rights of African Americans. This ruling was called the "*separate but equal doctrine.*" It gave rise to separate schools, stores, toilets, phone booths, graveyards and restaurants. The *separate but equal doctrine* stayed in effect until 1954.

Denied the Vote

In 1870, the 15th Amendment was passed. The 15th amendment gave all men the right to vote. But did this mean progress for African Americans? At first, the number of African American voters increased. But then in the late 1890s, the number of African American voters decreased dramatically. Why? In 1896, there were 130,344 African American voters in Louisiana. By 1900, two years after the passing of a "grandfather clause," there were 5,320 African American voters.

The grandfather clause was one way to stop African Americans from voting. The grandfather clause stated that if a

African American men line up along with white men to vote in 1867.

attacked when they tried to vote. Ben Tillman, a white Senator from South Carolina, said:

> "We have done our level best; we have scratched our heads to find out how we could eliminate the last one of them [African Americans].
>
> We stuffed ballot boxes. We shot them. We are not ashamed of it."[5]

African and white Americans knew that having the right to vote was very important. Without it, certain prejudiced white leaders would continue to take rights away from African Americans. The struggle was not over.

man's ancestors had voted on or before a certain date, then he could vote even if he couldn't read, write or pass other illegal voting tests. States that had the grandfather clause would pick a date such as 1866 when there had been no African American voters in that state. The result of the grandfather clause was that all white men, but no African Americans, could vote.

Some states had unfair reading tests. These tests were very hard, and white people did not have to take them in order to vote. In some cases, African Americans had to own land, or pay a poll tax or sum of money to vote. In most cases, whites did not have to do anything except show up to vote. Often, African Americans were kept away from the polls by force. Many were

Ben Tillman

5 *Before the Mayflower*, Lerone Bennett, 1982

ACTIVITY

1. Research the *Plessy v. Ferguson* case. Explain why you think the Supreme Court decided on *separate but equal*.

2. Interview older African Americans who grew up in the fifties while *separate but equal* was still the law. Find out how life was different for an African American student such as yourself under *separate but equal*.

CHAPTER 17 REVIEW

Write your answers on a separate piece of paper.

VOCABULARY TO KNOW

Use context clues or a dictionary to help you write definitions for the following words:

1. segregation
2. professional
3. media
4. tactic
5. lynch
6. lodge
7. oppress
8. degrade

Thinking Critically

1. Define segregation and list some reasons for its development.

2. In your own words, explain the different ways segregation affected the lives of both African and white Americans.

3. Describe the progress African Americans made between the end of the Civil War and the beginning of the 1900s.

Writing

4. Make a poster that shows the similarities and differences in thinking between Booker T. Washington and W.E.B. DuBois. Use the library for your research. Include pictures of both men on the poster (drawings, tracings, copied photos, collage).

5. Explain the statement on p. 123: "The Reconstruction period had taught these white leaders a lesson…" Explain this statement in your own words.

6. Write a paragraph giving your analysis of how Jim Crow laws could have created misunderstanding, fear, and harm for many years to come.

18 AFRICAN AMERICANS MOVE INTO PROMINENCE

EARLY 1900s

 Madame C.J. Walker created the first line of cosmetics for African American women. In the 1900s, African Americans were finally seen as consumers for the first time. Walker's company made her one of the most prominent African American businesswomen of the twentieth century. Walker was also the first African American woman to open a bank.

This symbol originated in Western Nigeria and was created to look like a carved pattern on a Yoruba ivory Jug.

Against great odds, Madame C. J. Walker became a wealthy businesswoman in the early 1900s.

As the country grew, African Americans made progress as the fight for equality continued. But equality did not come quickly.

African Americans were treated unfairly in the media. They were degraded and stereotyped in magazines, newspapers and nursery rhymes. They were made to look dangerous and foolish in cartoons, movies and on the radio. Millions of Americans read the newspapers, listened to the radio and watched cartoons and movies. Media stereotypes became part of shaping attitudes against African Americans.

Still, many African Americans made progress. They did this through hard work against great odds. In 1865, only about one out of twenty African Americans could read and write.[1] Most white slaveowners had not allowed them to learn. African Americans recognized that it was very important to be able to read and write. Thousands of African Americans, young and old, went to the new freedom schools after the Civil War. Often, children, their parents and their grandparents would sit in the same classroom to learn to read and write. By 1900, about one out of two African Americans could read and write.[2]

 African Americans were constantly degraded and stereotyped in magazines and newspapers. This helped to shape the attitudes of European Americans towards African Americans.

1 *Before the Mayflower*, Lerone Bennett, 1982

2 *Ibid.*

Between the end of the Civil War and 1900, many new church groups, African American colleges, lodges and business leagues were established. African Americans continued to develop their own institutions. They worked together to make life better. As a result, the number of African American businesses and professionals grew quickly. By 1900, there were more than 20,000 African American teachers and more than 2,000 African American doctors in the United States. There were more than 700 African American lawyers and 300 African American journalists. More than 800 African American inventors had registered patents by this time.

African Americans operated and owned new retail stores, banks, hotels, newspapers and insurance companies. Although there were many forces working against African Americans, African Americans made steady gains.

Forced segregation in this country lasted from 1877 to the 1960s. Segregation, however, was not profitable for the rest of the country. A country cannot develop well when millions of its citizens are abused and held back from fully contributing their skills and talents. And those who discriminate against African Americans are degraded by their actions. Inequality hurt the economic well-being of many United States citizens, holding them back and harming the country. The harm was more than economic, it was harmful to all people.

In 1900, Booker T. Washington and other supporters of black African Americans self-help formed the National Negro Business League.

ACTIVITY

The people on pages 133-134 made many contributions to America against great odds during the period of segregation. Use library resources to write a report on one of these people.

JOHN HOPE

MARY MCLEOD BETHUNE

W.E.B. DUBOIS

DR. DANIEL H. WILLIAMS

ACTIVITY

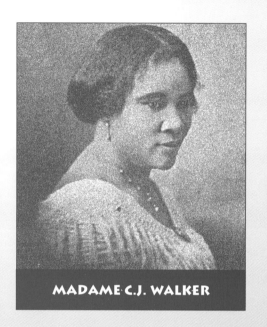

MADAME C.J. WALKER

BOOKER T. WASHINGTON

JAMES WELDON JOHNSON

IDA B. WELLS

CHAPTER 18 REVIEW

Write your answers on a separate piece of paper.

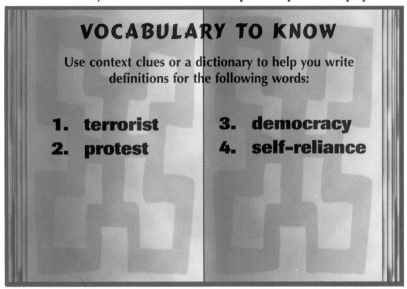

VOCABULARY TO KNOW

Use context clues or a dictionary to help you write definitions for the following words:

1. terrorist
2. protest

3. democracy
4. self-reliance

Thinking Critically

1. In your own words, describe how African Americans moved into prominence in the early 1900s. Give examples.

2. How could false stereotypes and cartoons in newspapers, magazines, movies, and nursery rhymes be degrading to African Americans? Why might media people have presented such stereotypes?

Writing

3. Pretend that you are an African American journalist or movie maker in 1900. You want to be interesting, but also want to let people know how inequality can hurt everyone in the country. Write an outline for your article or movie. (You may wish to do this activity alone or in a small group.)

4. Write an essay explaining why education is needed for all people. Talk about their personal feelings, economics, and other topics.

5. Write a persuasive composition entitled, "Segregation Hurt America." Include at least two examples of how segregation hurt America and explain each example.

THE STRUGGLE AGAINST SEGREGATION: MORAL, LEGAL AND POLITICAL BATTLES

1900-1930

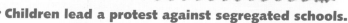

◈ **Children lead a protest against segregated schools.**

This symbol originated in Congo, Kinshasa and was created to look like a carved pattern on a Bushongo wooden drum.

Between 1900 and 1930, segregation and discrimination worsened in America. Violence toward African Americans increased. Innocent people were lynched and burned. Their homes were set on fire by mobs. The Ku Klux Klan, a white terrorist group, grew in size. Between 1900 and 1922, more than 1,300 African Americans were lynched.

In 1918, World War I ended. African Americans who served in the war returned to the United States. They had fought and died just like their fellow white soldiers. They had helped to win a war for democracy. They were ready for equality at home.

But returning African American soldiers did not like what they found at home. They found little democracy in America for African Americans. Many people fought against this unequal treatment by forming groups that worked to gain equal treatment for all.

 The Ku Klux Klan used violence illegally to try and force African Americans to give up their struggle for liberty and equality.

Many African Americans were lynched before the NAACP could end violent lynchings and race riots.

The National Association for the Advancement of Colored People (NAACP) and the Urban League were two groups who fought for change. The National Association of Colored Women, though less prominent than the NAACP or the Urban League, was another.

The NAACP was formed in 1909. It worked to stop lynchings and race riots. It fought segregation laws in the courts. The NAACP tried to prove that such laws went against the Constitution. The NAACP had a staff of African American and white lawyers. They defended African American people who were unfairly accused of crimes. The NAACP still does this work today.

Thousands of African Americans had moved to Northern cities such as St. Louis in the early 1900s. They were looking for better jobs. Sometimes factories would hire African American workers and pay them lower wages than whites.

African Americans Work in Peace

In 1917, a bloody race riot took place in East St. Louis, Missouri. White workers became angry and attacked African American workers and their families. Many African Americans were killed. Six thousand were driven from their homes. The whites feared that African Americans would take "their" jobs. The NAACP held a parade in New York City to protest this attack. The 10,000 people who joined to walk in that parade walked in silence and peace.

In 1910, the Urban League was formed. It worked for better housing in the cities. It tried to end unfair hiring practices. Many white people worked in this group and in other groups. Some helped by donating or raising money.

In 1820, there were ten African American newspapers in America. In 1890, there were 154. Between 1900 and 1930, many more newspapers such as the *Chicago Defender* and magazines such as *Crisis* were started.[1] They printed news that was of high interest

---

1 Others were *Opportunity, Guardian, The Messenger,* and *Negro World.*

NAACP Anti-Lynching Campaign

Association. Mr. Garvey talked about racial pride and self-reliance. He started many African American-owned businesses.

Marcus Garvey did not think America would ever be fair to African Americans. He wanted a group of African Americans to start a new government in

to African Americans. They gave points of view that were not printed in other papers.

Many great African American leaders lived during the early 1900s. Among these were Dr. W.E.B. DuBois, William Monroe Trotter, Ida B. Wells, Robert Abbott, Booker T. Washington and Mary McLeod Bethune. Each of these people fought segregation and discrimination. They and many others worked for equal justice.

In 1920, a man named Marcus Garvey formed a group called the Universal Negro Improvement

Africa. Although this did not happen, about one million people did join his group. "Up you mighty race," he thundered, "You can do what you will." Garvey did a great deal to increase a sense of dignity among African Americans. His philosophy of pride in being African rang true with many African Americans.

Segregation was still a fixed part of American life in the early 1900s, but African Americans made cultural, political and economic gains.[2] Segregation was being attacked in all areas of American life.

2 a. cultural gains: In the field of arts, music, literature. See Chapter 22, "The Harlem Renaissance." b. political gains: such as forming new groups that fought for change: electing black officials, fighting for justice in the courts. c. economic gains: There were many new small and large African American businesses in the South and North. A few men and women became millionaires such as Madame C. J. Walker. By 1928, African Americans owned 50 banks. They also owned 25 insurance companies worth $2 billion.

Cheated by white shipowners who had sold him worn-out vessels for his Black Star Steamship Line, black nationalist Marcus Garvey was indicted, tried, and convicted. His "crime" was using the mails to fraudulently advertise his ships. He was later pardoned by President Coolidge, who had him deported. Garvey died in London in 1941 a poor man, but one who had inspired millions.

Marcus Garvey was born in Jamaica. His movement for African nationalism and pride appealed to millions. "Up, you mighty race," were his famous words calling African Americans to rise up in black pride.

ACTIVITY

1. Research an African American leader during the time period of 1900-1930. Find out what he or she stood for. Find out his or her philosophy and beliefs. Write a description of your leader's philosophy. Then give your own opinion of that philosophy. Do you agree or disagree? Why?

2. Pretend that you are a strong African American leader at this time. Write a speech to express your own philosophy on what African Americans should do to get ahead. Present your speech to the class.

CHAPTER 19 REVIEW

Write your answers on a separate piece of paper.

VOCABULARY TO KNOW

Use context clues or a dictionary to help you write definitions for the following words:

1. terrorist
2. protest
3. democracy
4. self-reliance
5. mob

Thinking Critically

1. List some examples of violence against African Americans during the period of segregation.

2. Name three groups that worked for the development of African Americans during the early 1900s and explain what they did.

3. Explain Marcus Garvey's philosophy. Why was it appealing? Why?

Writing

4. Write a biography of one of the leaders of this period. Draw or photocopy his or her picture to include in your report.

5. Make a poster about the National Association for the Advancement of Colored People, the Urban League, and the Universal Negro Improvement Association. Design your poster so it includes the following:

   ❧ what each group did in this period
   ❧ what injustices each group fought against
   ❧ what economic and political improvements each group worked for

20

AFRICAN AMERICANS IN THE SPANISH AMERICAN WAR

1898

 African American soldiers of the 9th Cavalry led the charge up San Juan Hill.

This symbol originated in Benin, Nigeria, and was created to look like a bronze sculpture design.

African Americans in the military never stopped fighting for America. They were involved in the Spanish American War from the very beginning. When the battleship *Maine* was sunk, twenty-two African American sailors died. After the U.S. declared war in 1898, thousands of Americans rushed to enlist. The war lasted only ten weeks.

During the Spanish American War, four African American units were part of the regular army, not the volunteer army. The four units had existed since the Civil War. These were the 24th and 25th Infantry (soldiers on foot) regiments, and the 9th and 10th Cavalry (soldiers on horses) regiments. Each of these units saw action in the Spanish American War. More than one hundred African American soldiers were made officers at this time.

African American soldiers fought at the battle of San Juan in Cuba along with Theodore Roosevelt and the Rough Riders. One eyewitness said that: "the Negro troops started the charge [up San Juan Hill] and, with the Rough Riders, routed the Spanish, causing them to retreat in disorder, leaving their dead and wounded behind." **1**

There are many other reports of the heroism of African American soldiers in the Spanish American War. Rough Rider Frank Knox said, "I joined a troop of the Tenth Cavalry and for a time fought with them shoulder to shoulder, and injustice to the Colored race I must say that I never saw braver men anywhere. Some of those who rushed up the hill [San Juan Hill] will live in my memory forever." **2**

Four African American soldiers of the Tenth Cavalry received the Congressional Medal for bravery in Cuba. Others had excellent records in this war.

The 10th Cavalry saved the Rough Riders at San Juan Hill.

---

1 *Eyewitness: The Negro in American History,* William L. Katz, 1967

2 Ibid

When the Spanish American War was over, African American soldiers did not receive equal treatment or the kind of honors they expected. A few certificates of merit were awarded giving a $2.00 per month increase in pay. Men who had been officers during the war were demoted and returned to their original ranks. Some African American soldiers who had shown great ability or bravery were put into one of four African American regiments of the U.S. Volunteer Infantry as lieutenants. In about six months, this Volunteer Infantry was disbanded.

The Regular Army had only one African American officer, Lt. Charles Young. African American troops were led by white officers. Finally, the Volunteer Infantry was reestablished. It had two African American regiments with African American officers. Some of these men had served in the Spanish American War. They were still volunteers, but had some hope of being part of the Regular Army.

These African American soldiers are boarding a ship that will carry them home from Santiago, Cuba, at the end of the war. They did not receive the honors that they had expected, and deserved when they went home.

◈ The African American soldiers from the 25th Infantry were responsible for capturing the first prisoners of the Spanish American War.

◈ African American soldiers fought in the Spanish American War alongside white soldiers. They were, however, treated differently. Here, African American soldiers are serving and cleaning up while white soldiers relax and have a meal.

ACTIVITY

RESEARCHING AND WRITING

1. Why might an African American man in 1898 have wanted to go to the Spanish American war? Write a letter home from the war explaining to your loved ones and friends why you wanted to go. Explain what you hope to accomplish.

2. Write a short play in two acts. In Act One, show what your regiment has done in the war. You will need to research this. In Act Two, argue with the white generals for equality. Maintain respect, but make your point. Perform your play for the class. You way wish to do this with a small group.

Write your answers on a separate piece of paper.

VOCABULARY TO KNOW

Use context clues or a dictionary to help you write definitions for the following words:

1. disband
2. cavalry
3. infantry

4. merit
5. demote
6. rank

Thinking Critically

1. Describe how African American soldiers participated in the success of the Spanish American War.

2. List the African American units that were part of the regular army during the Spanish American War. Tell whether each unit is made up of foot soldiers or soldiers on horses.

Writing

3. Pretend that you have just participated in the battle of San Juan Hill. Write a letter home describing what happened.

4. Research and write a short biography of Lt. Charles Young.

AFRICAN AMERICANS IN WORLD WAR I

1917-1918

 The 369th regiment was one of three African American regiments to be awarded the Croix de Guerre. This French medal of honor is one of the highest awards given for bravery in battle.

This symbol originated in the Congo, Kinshasa, and was created to look like a Bushongo Raffia Pile Cotton Pattern.

It was said that World War I was fought to make the world safe for democracy. But African American soldiers found little democracy at home when the war ended. They still found discrimination in the armed forces, too. For the most part, African American soldiers were given the worst jobs with the lowest rank. They were rarely allowed to advance. Often, they served under prejudiced officers. Many times, they were called names and attacked by white soldiers. If they fought back, they were arrested.

African American soldiers and African American leaders in the U.S. learned many things during World War I. They learned that the war grew out of a struggle for power between some of the countries in Europe. Germany, France and England were three of these powerful countries. They also learned that each of these countries had colonies in Africa and Asia.

America had been a colony of England before the Revolutionary War. England still had many colonies in Africa and Asia by the time of World War I. So did France and Germany. People who lived in these African and Asian colonies were people of color.

They were treated very badly by their colonial rulers. Colonial rulers controlled the governments and businesses. The wealth they gained by doing this helped them to become even more powerful. The wealth did not go back to the communities in Africa and Asia, so the local economies did not grow.

Some African Americans thought that the way Africans and Asians were being treated in these colonies was similar to their treatment in America. They were starting to gain a global view of the world. They began looking at the events of the whole world to see how they fit together.[1] But in spite of what African American soldiers learned, they remained very patriotic. They fought bravely for America.

 African American soldiers fought bravely for America, despite the ways in which allied countries mistreated their African and Asian colonies.

[1] W.E.B. DuBois had a global view. He organized a Pan African Congress at the end of the war (1918). This brought together people of African ancestry. There were 57 delegates from around the world. They talked about ending mistreatment of people of color by working together.

During World War I, about 370,000 African American soldiers and 1,400 officers went overseas. More than half went to France. Many were assigned to service units rather than combat units. Those who served in combat units were in many battles. Many won honors for their valor. Henry Johnson and Needham Roberts were the first two African Americans to win France's Croix de Guerre. This is the highest French war honor. It means "Cross of War." The 369th regiment set a record of 191 days on the firing line. This was more than any other American regiment. During this time they did not lose a single prisoner or a single foot of ground. Three African American regiments were awarded the Croix de Guerre. The 371st regiment won 121 French and twenty-seven American Distinguished Service Crosses.

 The 369th regiment returns from Europe after 191 days on the firing line without losing any ground or a single prisoner. Many African American troops were dispatched abroad during World War I.

After the war, U.S. General Pershing said to the 92nd Division as it was ready to leave France: "I want you officers and soldiers of the 92nd Division to know that the 92nd Division stands second to none in the record you have made since your arrival in France . . . The American public has every reason to be proud of that record . . . ."[2]

During the war, the National Association for the Advancement of Colored People (NAACP) led a successful effort to have the army train African American soldiers as officers. But the army said that they must be trained separately from white soldiers. By 1917, the Negro Officer Training Camp at Des Moines, Iowa, trained more than 600 captains and lieutenants. The 370th Regiment was led almost totally by African American officers. It fought in the last battle of World War I.

This wounded World War I hero has returned from Europe. He is warmly received in his hometown, Harlem, N.Y., but many other Americans don't appreciate the sacrifices of an African American soldier.

The regiments in World War I were segregated. These African American soldiers are returning home after the last battles of the war.

2 *Eyewitness: The Negro in American History*, William Katz, 1967

ACTIVITY

1. Pretend you are a member of this World War I regiment. Research some more accomplishments of African American regiments in World War I. Write a description of your regiment's accomplishments based on historical fact. Write also about daily life and your expectations.

2. Pretend you are General Pershing about to address the 92nd Division as it prepares to leave France at the end of World War I. Write a short speech to deliver to your troops.

CHAPTER 21 REVIEW

Write your answers on a separate piece of paper.

VOCABULARY TO KNOW

Use context clues or a dictionary to help you write definitions for the following words:

1. patriotic
2. valor
3. global
4. mistreated
5. colony
6. local economy

Thinking Critically

1. List some observations made by African American soldiers and African American leaders in the United States from their experiences in World War I.

2. Describe the honors won by African American soldiers in World War I.

Writing

3. Explain what is meant by the term *global view*. Tell how World War I caused many African Americans to develop a global view.

4. Explain why a *colonial* system may lead to problems in any age or time.

THE HARLEM RENAISSANCE
1920-1929

1. James Baldwin (author)
2. Marcus Garvey (reformer)
3. Charles Drew (Biologist)
4. Roland Hayes (concert performer)
5. Carter G. Woodson (historian)
6. Alain Locke (author)
7. Marion Anderson (opera singer)
8. Paul Robeson (actor, singer)
9. Duke Ellington (musician)
10. Langston Hughes (poet)
11. W.E.B DuBois (reformer)
12. Dr. Daniel H. Williams (surgeon)
13. Bessie Smith (blues singer)
14. Charles Gilpin (actor)
15. James Weldon Johnson (poet)
16. Zora Neale Hurston (novelist)
17. Aaron Douglas (artist)
18. Arna Bontemps (educator)

This symbol originated in the Congo, Kinshasa, and was created to look like a Bushongo woven wall matting design.

1. Louis Armstrong (trumpeter)
2. Ferdinand "Jellyroll" Morton (pianist-composer)
3. Sidney Bechet (clarinetist)
4. Members of the Black Intelligentsia (from left to right) poet Langston Hughest, sociologist Charles S. Johnson, sociologist E. Franklin Frazier, novelist Rudolph Fisher, and Hubert Delany

The Harlem Renaissance took place between 1920 and 1929. It was a time of great creative work involving many artists, writers, musicians and performers. It was a creative renaissance of African culture. Harlem, a part of New York City, was the center of this activity. African Americans and African immigrants were cultural stars—writing, acting, painting, sculpting and forging new philosophies.

By 1920, a large number of African Americans lived in Harlem. The Renaissance came about because of a growing sense of African American pride. It also came about because Harlem was now a section of New York with its own elected leaders. The leaders were helping to develop this part of the city. They were interested in showing people there how to have more political control over their lives. All kinds of support came from these leaders and from the growing African American media.[1]

Many African American artists at this time had patrons, some of whom were white. Harlem came to be an exciting place for them to go. Night clubs in Harlem were showing all-African American talent to all-white segregated audiences. The time was exciting, and the talent seemed to center on Harlem.

The Harlem Renaissance is most known for its artists, writers and performers. It was also a period of reform. Men such as W.E.B. DuBois and Marcus Garvey worked to change laws and customs that harmed African

In the 1920s, Harlem, New York, became the black capital of the world.

1 *Crisis Magazine, Opportunity, Negro World* and *The Messenger* published the work of writers and artists.

American people. They also worked to increase African American awareness of Africa. Each of these men was part of the rebirth and revival of the growth and self-esteem of African Americans.

Great thinkers of the 1920s met with artists, writers and musicians in Africa and Europe. They shared ideas and talents. Out of this sharing came the Pan-African Movement. The Pan-African Movement supplied a link between African people in America and the African land of their ancestors. W.E.B. DuBois helped to start this movement.

Alain Locke came up with a term to describe the proud, talented, confident African American of the Harlem Renaissance. He called this the *New Negro*. He wrote a book called *The New Negro*. In his book, he wrote about the exciting changes that were happening as African Americans became educated and self-confident.

Langston Hughes, a writer and poet, was also very vocal. He wrote about the new appreciation of African and African American talent. And he wrote negatively about African Americans who, with economic success, suddenly thought only white writing, art and music could be best.

The Harlem Renaissance was an explosion of the African spirit in all the arts and philosophy. African Americans all across the country were proud to see the U.S. begin to show proper respect to African American artists, musicians, writers and leaders. For this time, Harlem was the place to be.

The Harlem Renaissance ended with bad times—the Depression. People who were patrons of African American artists could not continue to support these artists. They had no money to do so. Publishers stopped using African American writers. The African American "vogue" was fading, but only temporarily.

Arna Bontemps was a writer who was part of the Harlem Renaissance. In 1970 he said, "The Harlem Renaissance was an awakening of creative energy among black Americans, but its influence was so electrical it began to reach a generation of Americans of many kinds who were glad to play into its power source. . . ." On the following page are parts of poems by four well-known writers of this period. Writers use words to express feelings and thoughts. What do you think each writer was trying to tell you?

Alain Locke's book, **The New Negro**, was the start of the Harlem Renaissance.

The following poems were composed by writers in the Harlem Renaissance.

THE NEGRO SPEAKS OF RIVERS

(1902-1969)
LANGSTON HUGHES

I've known rivers:
I've known rivers ancient as the world and older than the
flow of human blood in human veins.
My soul has grown deep like the rivers.
I bathed in the Euphrates when dawns were young.
I built my hut near the Congo and it lulled me to sleep.
I looked upon the Nile and raised the pyramids above it .
I've heard the singing of the Mississippi when Abe Lincoln
went down to New Orleans, and I've seen its muddy bosom
turn all golden in the sunset.
I've know rivers:
Ancient, dusky rivers.
My soul has grown deep like the rivers.

"THE WHITE HOUSE"

CLAUDE McKAY (1889-1948)

Your door is shut against my tightened face,
And I am sharp as steel with discontent;
But I possess the courage and the grace
To bear my anger proudly and unbent.
The pavement slabs burn loose beneath my feet,
A chafing savage, down the decent street;
And passion rends my vitals as I pass,
Where boldly shines your shuttered door of glass.
Oh, I must search for wisdom every hour,
Deep in my wrathful bosom sore and raw,
And find in it the superhuman power
To hold me to the letter of your law!
Oh, I must keep my heart inviolate
Against the potent poison of your hate.

OLD LEM

STERLING A. BROWN
(1901-1989)

They weigh the cotton
They store the corn
We only good enough
To work the rows
They keep the books
We got to be grateful
For being cheated;
Wippersnapper clerks
Call us out of our name
We got to say mister
To spindling boys
They make our figures
Turn somersets
We buck in the middle
Say "Thank you, sah."
They don't come by ones
They don't come by two
But they come by the tens.

INCIDENT, 1925

(For Eric Walrond)
COUNTEE CULLEN (1903-1946)

Once riding in old Baltimore.
Heart-filled, head filled with glee,
I saw a Baltimorean
Keep looking straight at me.
Now I was eight and very small,
And he was no whit bigger,
And so I smiled, but he poked out
His tongue, and called me, "Nigger."
I saw a lot of Baltimore.
From May until December;
Of all the things that happened there,
That's all that I remember.

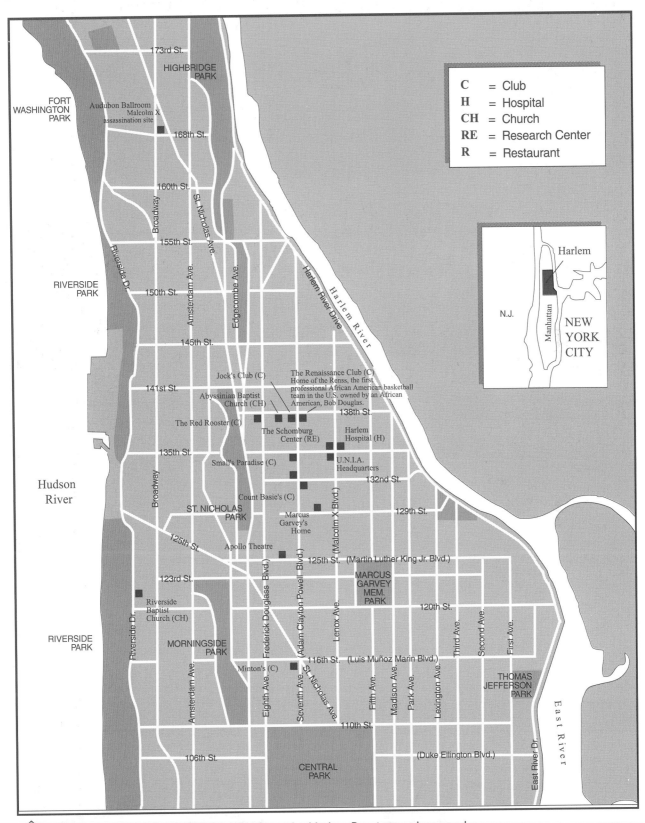

Legend:

C	=	Club
H	=	Hospital
CH	=	Church
RE	=	Research Center
R	=	Restaurant

173rd St.

HIGHBRIDGE PARK

FORT WASHINGTON PARK

Audubon Ballroom Malcolm X assassination site

168th St.

160th St.

155th St.

RIVERSIDE PARK

150th St.

145th St.

141st St.

Jock's Club (C)

The Renaissance Club (C)
Home of the Renss, the first professional African American basketball team in the U.S. owned by an African American, Bob Douglas.

Abyssinian Baptist Church (CH)

138th St.

The Red Rooster (C)

The Schomburg Center (RE)

Harlem Hospital (H)

135th St.

Small's Paradise (C)

U.N.I.A. Headquarters

132nd St.

Hudson River

Count Basie's (C)

ST. NICHOLAS PARK

Marcus Garvey's Home

129th St.

125th St.

Apollo Theatre

125th St. (Martin Luther King Jr. Blvd.)

123rd St.

Riverside Baptist Church (CH)

MARCUS GARVEY MEM. PARK

120th St.

RIVERSIDE PARK

MORNINGSIDE PARK

Minton's (C)

116th St. (Luis Muñoz Marin Blvd.)

THOMAS JEFFERSON PARK

East River

110th St.

106th St.

(Duke Ellington Blvd.)

CENTRAL PARK

Broadway

St. Nicholas Ave.

Amsterdam Ave.

Edgecombe Ave.

Harlem River Drive

Harlem River

Riverside Dr.

Frederick Douglass Blvd.

(Adam Clayton Powell Blvd.)

Seventh Ave.

St. Nicholas Ave.

Lenox Ave.

(Malcolm X Blvd.)

Fifth Ave.

Madison Ave.

Park Ave.

Lexington Ave.

Third Ave.

Second Ave.

First Ave.

East River Dr.

Eighth Ave.

Amsterdam Ave.

Harlem

N.J.

Manhattan

NEW YORK CITY

Harlem, part of New York City, was where the Harlem Renaissance happened.

ACTIVITY

Zora Neal Hurston

Paul Robeson

Duke Ellington

Marcus Garvey

Langston Hughes

LIFT EVERY VOICE AND SING

1. Choose one of the writers, musicians, actors and reformers of the Harlem Renaissance, shown below, and write a biography. Research your subject.

ZORA NEAL HURSTON   PAUL ROBESON   DUKE ELLINGTON
MARCUS GARVEY   LANGSTON HUGHES

2. This poem and song was written by James Weldon Johnson. At the time, it was called the **_Negro National Anthem_**. Read the poem. Get a recording of the song. With a small group, sing it for your class and teach it to them.

LIFT EVERY VOICE AND SING

Lift every voice and sing, Till earth and heaven ring,
Ring with the harmonies of liberty;
Let our rejoicing rise High as the listening skies,
Let it resound loud as the rolling sea.
Sing a song full of the faith that the dark past has taught us;
Sing a song full of the hope that it brought us;
Facing the rising sun of our new day begun,
Let us march on til' victory is won.

CHAPTER 22 REVIEW

Write your answers on a separate piece of paper.

VOCABULARY TO KNOW

Use context clues or a dictionary to help you write definitions for the following words:

1. reformer
2. patron
3. self-esteem
4. renaissance
5. vogue
6. depression

Thinking Critically

1. Describe the Harlem Renaissance. Why did it begin? Why did it end? Include the dates it lasted.

2. Describe the types of support that African American artists, writers and performers had during the Harlem Renaissance.

Writing

3. Select a person from the Harlem Renaissance and do the following:

a. If you chose a writer, find a selection of his or her work to read to the class. Spend time practicing it.

b. If you selected a musician or an actor, find a recording to play for the class. Use the library, or bring the recording from home.

c. If you selected a reformer, tell what reform(s) her or she sought.

CHAPTER

23

THE GREAT DEPRESSION AND THE AFRICAN AMERICAN WORKER

1929-1939

 A long line of jobless and homeless men wait to get a free dinner at New York's Municipal Lodging House in the winter of 1933.

This symbol originated in Ghana, and was created to look like a beaten pattern on an Ashanti bronze urn.

In 1929, the United States was faced with a time known as the Depression. The stock market crashed. People lost their savings in the crash. Factories and banks closed. Jobs were scarce. Food prices rose so high that many people could not buy food. They had to wait in bread lines and soup kitchens to eat at all.

African Americans were hit very hard in the Depression. They were often the "last hired and the first fired." Those who had the same levels of skill as white people usually lost their jobs first. African Americans lost a third of the jobs they had held before the Depression.

African American leaders in the 1920s asked white leaders such as Samuel Gompers, head of the American Federation of Labor (AFL), a union, to allow African American workers to join the white unions. Gompers would not agree. The union did not want African American workers competing with white American workers for jobs.

African American leaders such as Asa Philip Randolph formed unions

Asa Philip Randolph

of African American workers. These were the *United Negro Traders* and the *Brotherhood of Sleeping Car Porters*. But still, white workers were given jobs first. Many European Americans took low-skilled jobs away from African American workers. African American workers with high levels of skill were denied jobs because they were not in the white unions.

Then, four things happened to change some of this.

First, a union called the *Congress of Industrial Organizations* (CIO) was formed by John L. Lewis. He welcomed African American workers to join. By 1940, about 200,000 African American workers were members.

Second, African American people were gaining strength in politics. Some two million African Americans had moved north since 1915. There were parts of some cities in the North that had mostly African American voters. They could elect leaders of their choice. White leaders were starting to listen to demands of African Americans. Also, President Franklin D. Roosevelt asked African American leaders such as Robert C. Weaver and Mary McLeod Bethune to be his advisors on race relations. They were called his "Black Cabinet" or the "Black Brain Trust."

Third, the call for racial unity had steadily increased by the 1930s. There was a *Black Buying Power* movement. Its slogan was: "Don't Buy Where You Can't Work." There were many pickets in front of war plants that would not hire African American workers. A. Philip Randolph, thought of as the father of the African American labor movement, told President Roosevelt that he would march on Washington with 100,000 workers. President Roosevelt wanted to avoid this, so he set up an agency that would try to protect the rights of all workers. It was called the *Fair Employment Practices Commission*. This was the first act by the government to help African American workers since Reconstruction.

Fourth, *The National Association for the Advancement of Colored People* (NAACP) was winning Supreme Court battles against discrimination. The Court banned the grandfather clause (see Chapter 17). Cases were won against residential segregation. Cases were won against college segregation. Cases were won to make African American and European American teachers have equal pay.

Although the Depression was very hard for African Americans, they came through it and made gains. There were now more national groups to speak out and fight unfair treatment. Equal rights for all Americans was becoming a reality even though it was taking time.

The Memorial Day Massacre of 1937

The following first-person account is taken from *Eyewitness: The Negro in American History*, by William L. Katz, Pitman Publishers, 1964:

> "[One of the most dramatic events in the rise of the CIO's United Steel Workers Union was the Memorial Day Massacre of Sunday, May 30, 1937. A parade of strikers was driven off by police bullets outside the Republic Steel Plant of Chicago. Ten workers were killed.]
>
> [A Negro striker] On that Sunday we marched out of the plant with signs. Lots of us were singing songs and laughing. I was in the front line. All of a sudden the cops started shooting. When they started, I ran to my extreme right, then west, then I made an "L" turn to the south. All the time, bullets were going right past my face.
>
> When I looked up I saw a guy right on top of the plant training his gun on us. I couldn't tell whether it was a machine gun, 'cause I was anxious to get out of the line of fire. I could see the police in my path, the way I was running, so I turned around toward Sam's Place. I ran to a car and started to duck into it. A bullet whizzed by and lodged right above the right fender. Boy, I shake now when I think that if I hadn't ducked I'd have been shot in the head. I finally made it into the car and was driven to Sam's Place.

[The wife of the one Negro killed that day.] He was told to go to the meeting that Sunday. He was on the front line and was one of the first to get hurt. I have his clothes here. You can see where he was shot in the back. His hat is bloody. He sure was beat terrible. His life was really lost for the CIO, whether he understood it or not. I do hope his loss will help others who live."

 Young people picketed, protesting peacefully, in 1938 at the King Farm outside Morrisville, Pennsylvania. They wanted African Americans to be able to join unions. Protests of places that used all-white unions for labor continued.

ACTIVITY

1. Reread the first-person account of the Memorial Day Massacre in the chapter. Now, read it aloud as a dramatic reading. Think about the emotion in the account.

2. Write a sequel to the account. Tell what happened later to the workers who were not killed. Read your sequel aloud as a dramatic reading.

CHAPTER 23 REVIEW

Write your answers on a separate piece of paper.

VOCABULARY TO KNOW

Use context clues or a dictionary to help you write definitions for the following words:

1. race relations
2. picket

3. unity
4. massacre
5. union

Thinking Critically

1. In a paragraph, tell how the Depression affected African Americans.

2. List four things that happened to help African Americans during the Depression.

Writing

3. Pretend you are living during the Depression. Make a diary entry about how the Depression is affecting you and your family. Include information about things that are happening to change some of this.

4. Using library resources, find the names of African American leaders who served as President Franklin D. Roosevelt's advisors on race relations. Write a short report on one of these individuals. Explain his or her attitude and contributions to racial unity.

AFRICAN AMERICANS IN WORLD WAR II

1941-1945

 Hundreds of African American were pilots in the Air Force during World War II. Shown above is Captain Turner of the 332nd Fighter Group, which flew in Italy.

This symbol originated in Northern Nigeria and was created to look like a mud wall relief design.

In the early morning of December 7, 1941, Japanese planes attacked the U.S. Naval Base at Pearl Harbor, Hawaii. Dorie Miller, a young sailor, dropped the laundry he had been collecting and ran onto the deck. In the midst of the bombing, he pulled his wounded captain out of the direct line of fire. Then he jumped to action behind a machine gun. He had never fired a machine gun before that day. He fired at the attacking planes. An officer had to order him to leave the ship because it was sinking.

Dorie Miller was America's first hero of World War II. The navy credited him with shooting down four Japanese planes. He received the Navy Cross ". . .for distinguished devotion to duty, extraordinary courage, and disregard for his own personal safety..." Miller served as a mess attendant. At the time, this was the only position open to African American sailors.

More Than 1,000,000 African Americans

More than one million African Americans entered the armed forces and served in World War II. At first, they were barred from some units, such as the marines and the air corps. After a while, men served in every branch of the armed forces. Women were army nurses, WACS and WAVES. There were 7,000 African American officers. Four African American officers commanded merchant marine ships. Some led battalions and air squadrons. Others led artillery units.

African Americans faced much discrimination in the U.S. armed forces. Once again, they saw that fighting for democracy did not change the racism at home. African American soldiers were segregated. They were

World War II hero Dorie Miller

IN OUR OWN IMAGE

 General Benjamin O. Davis, Jr.

in Tuskegee, Alabama, became famous for their courage in the air. By 1945, almost 600 African American pilots were flying.

Overseas, African Americans served as soldiers, sailors, officers, airmen, engineers, truck drivers, laborers, doctors, nurses and journalists. African American units fought in tanks, the infantry, or any other way they were allowed to fight. African American units were among those who freed Nazi prisoners from concentration camps in Germany.

At home, however, war plants were turning away African American workers when the war started. They

often called names. At times, they were attacked. If they fought back, they often were jailed. All their commanding officers were white. Segregation did not end in the armed forces until 1948, three years after the war was over.

Hundreds of African American soldiers and entire units won honors and medals in World War II. They fought in Europe, Asia, the Pacific Islands and North Africa. They were in all the major battles, winning high praise from several generals. The highest ranking African American officer was Colonel Benjamin O. Davis, Jr. He was a pilot who won many medals.

African American fighting units fought bravely in spite of discrimination. The Tuskegee Flyers, African American pilots who trained at a segregated base

African Americans were still discriminated against at home. They were allowed to risk their lives in battle, but often not allowed to hold jobs at home.

hired white women, instead, when there were not enough white men. After A. Philip Randolph threatened President Roosevelt with a march on Washington,[1] some of this changed.

Many African Americans moved North. There, plants and factories were more willing to hire them than in the South.

Other African Americans such as Dr. Charles Drew helped in different ways. Drew was in charge of the Red Cross blood bank. He invented a way to store blood plasma in a dry state. Blood could then be sent overseas. It saved the lives of many wounded soldiers.

World War II veterans returned home to find a shortage of homes and jobs. African American veterans also found racial discrimination. Discrimination was what they had been helping to destroy in Europe and Asia. It was hard to accept unfair treatment at home now that foreign enemies had been beaten. If the idea of a Nazi "master race"[2] was wrong for our enemies, it was wrong for America, too.

There was no going back. African Americans, without jobs and homes, were not about to give up another fight. The discrimination at home set off the beginning of the Civil Rights Movement. It would take time, but change would come.

 Dr. Charles Drew

[1] *See Besson 23, "The Great Depression and the African American Worker"*

[2] *World War II, the leaders of Germany said that the Germans were a "master race."*

ACTIVITY

1. Research African American fighting units in World War II. Pick one that interests you, and write a newspaper account of their achievements. Pretend that you are publishing your story the day they return from the war.

2. By yourself or with a small group, make a poster of jobs done by African Americans during World War II. Draw pictures to illustrate each.

Write your answers on a separate piece of paper.

VOCABULARY TO KNOW

Use context clues or a dictionary to help you write definitions for the following words:

1. **extraordinary**
2. **barred**
3. **racism**
4. **plasma**
5. **fighting unit**

Thinking Critically

1. Describe the contributions made by African Americans to help the war effort.

2. Name three African Americans, a doctor, a colonel and a mess attendant, who helped the war effort.

Writing

3. Pretend you are an African American soldier just returning from European combat in World War II. Write a letter to a relative in another state telling how it feels to be back home. Describe some of the problems you encountered upon your return.

THE CIVIL RIGHTS MOVEMENT
1950-1970

 On August 28, 1963, demonstrators walked from the Washington Monument to the Lincoln Memorial for the March on Washington to demand equal rights for all African Americans.

This symbol originated in Ghana, and was created to look like an Ashanti bronze gold weight.

The Civil Rights Movement of the 1950s and 1960s was a brave and dramatic battle with "soldiers" on many fronts. Men, women and children marched, debated and protested in the courts, the streets and in classrooms all across the country to make the United States live up to its promise of freedom and equality for all.

Participants in the Civil Rights movement at first seemed to share the same vision of freedom. But no two people think exactly alike. At times, differences in values and ways of doing things led to disagreements among civil rights workers.

One disagreement among people fighting for civil rights was between those who believed in nonviolent protest and others who felt that fighting back violently was the only way to get equal rights. Organizations such as the NAACP and SCLC (Southern Christian Leadership Conference) were at the forefront of the nonviolent protests. These groups held sit-ins, boycotts and marches. They also began lawsuits to try to change America peacefully. On the other hand, nationalist groups such as the Black Panthers and the Nation of Islam (also called the Black Muslims) insisted that a violent revolution was needed to force society to change.

While peaceful protests were held in some cities, race riots erupted in others. These riots often began in response to acts of violence by whites or the police in which African Americans were hurt or killed. The riots were fueled by the anger and frustration of people living in many poor urban areas. Businesses and neighborhoods were destroyed by fires and looting. Hundreds of people were arrested. Many were hurt, some were killed. In several cities, the National Guard was called in to help stop the fighting.

Malcolm X

Many African Americans hoped to find one leader who could bring together the ideas of all their people. For some, that leader was Malcolm X. Malcolm X was a spokesperson for the Nation of Islam, a religious group. At the beginning of the 1960s, Malcolm X inspired many who agreed that African Americans must fight back for equality "through any means necessary."

However, after returning from a religious pilgrimage to the Islamic holy city of Mecca, Malcolm X stopped believing that all white men were devils. He said that it was people's actions, not their skin color, that made them good or bad. Malcolm X was a brilliant speaker. He spoke about the need for African people to unite. He was religious and moral. Malcolm X spoke out strongly against white exploitation of African Americans. He believed that African Americans should not be dependent on white Americans.

This new way of thinking led him into a bitter conflict with Black Muslim leader, Elijah Muhammad. In 1964, Malcolm X broke away from the Nation of Islam and formed his own group, the Organization of Afro-American Unity. He continued to speak out against discrimination. In 1965, Malcolm X was

Malcolm X

shot and killed while speaking at a rally in Harlem in New York City. His death triggered more acts of civil disobedience. Civil disobedience is when citizens choose deliberately to disobey laws to make a point or protest unjust laws and acts. Malcolm X's death, along with his words in life, made people think and begin to act against discrimination. Malcolm's was not the only voice, of course.

Dr. Martin Luther King Jr.

While traveling around this country giving speeches and organizing marches and boycotts, Dr. Martin Luther King, Jr., also started to become a strong voice. Dr. King believed that racism

Elijah Muhammad

Dr. Martin Luther King, Mrs. Rosa Parks, and David Boston at a freedom rally, June 1963

Alabama. She refused to give her seat on a bus to a white man. She was arrested.

Dr. King and other African American leaders organized a boycott of the buses as a nonviolent protest. The boycott hurt white bus company owners economically. Although it was cold and many people had to walk miles to get to their jobs, the boycott worked. People nationwide focused on the injustice of discrimination.

The nationwide focus grew during the 1960s. The March on Washington on August 28, 1963, was a peaceful protest. Over 250,000 people, most but not all African Americans, marched to the Lincoln Memorial in Washington, D.C. Dr. Martin Luther King, Jr., gave his famous "I Have a Dream" speech.

But Dr. King did not have smooth sailing. Groups within the Civil Rights Movement disagreed with Dr. King when he began to include poor whites as well as African Americans in his work. Dr. King continued to work to end racism as well as poverty. Critics of Dr. King felt that the country would quickly forget about the issue of racial equality.

must end. However, he began to see the roots of race prejudice in this nation's economic problems. King saw that poverty touched all people. He saw that poverty made people afraid of any change. Poor people feared that change could cause them to lose their jobs or power. Dr. King began to believe that racism was caused as much by fear and greed as by ignorance and hate.

Still, Dr. King believed that civil disobedience would be needed to change discrimination. He wanted to work to help poor people. His position of non-violent protest made his opponents look bad anytime they used violence to try and stop him.

A woman named Rosa Parks started the civil disobedience and became a symbol of the Civil Rights Movement on December 1, 1955 in Montgomery,

 Dr. Martin Luther King, Jr.

For some, the emphasis of the movement shifted from the use of the ballot to the use of the bullet. Some new leaders called for "Black Power." Black Power meant that African Americans deserved full human and legal power, equal with whites. Many black power groups who worked to end discrimination were formed in the 1960s. Their pride in being black was their common theme. The SNCC (Student Nonviolent Coordinating Committee), Black Panthers, and Deacons for Defence were only a few of the black power groups that grew. With

They were strong, of course, but this debate among civil rights groups accelerated after Dr. King was assassinated in Memphis, Tennessee, in April 1968.

Black Power, Black Pride

Without the strong leadership of Martin Luther King, Jr,. and Malcolm X, the Civil Rights Movement almost stopped momentarily. For the first time in nearly thirteen years, the Civil Rights Movement was without a strong leader. Other, more radical voices began to be heard. Nonviolent protest philosophy was questioned.

 Black Panther national chairman Bobby Seale (left) and Huey Newton, defense minister (right)

the assassination of Malcolm X and Dr. King, leadership of the Civil Rights movement splintered. Most groups were nonviolent, but some used violence. Some groups, like the Black Panthers, believed they needed weapons to defend themselves from the violence of whites.

24th Amendment

In 1964, the Civil Rights Act was passed by Congress. It was the 24th Amendment to the U.S. Constitution. Discrimination and violating the civil rights of U.S. citizens, whatever their color, was illegal. In 1965, the Voting Rights Act was passed. It was a federal crime to stop African Americans from voting. Progress continued, but the struggle was not over for African Americans.

President Lyndon Johnson is signing the Civil Rights Act of 1957. Standing behind Johnson is Dr. Martin Luther King, Jr.

ACTIVITY

1. Research individuals and groups not discussed in this chapter who were a strong part of the Civil Rights Movement. Make a list of them and tell what two of these individuals or groups did.

2. Select one person or group from your list in number 1 (above). Write a report and make a poster to use as you share your report with the class.

3. Prepare a paper or speech that expresses your opinions on the ways the beliefs of Malcolm X, Dr. King and others are still important today. Be sure to draw conclusions about what you think we should still be doing to continue the progress of the Civil Rights Movement.

Write your answers on a separate piece of paper.

VOCABULARY TO KNOW

Use context clues or a dictionary to help you write definitions for the following words:

1. Civil Rights Movement
2. boycott
3. nationalism
4. riot

5. exploitation
6. Nation of Islam
7. civil disobedience
8. nonviolent protest

Thinking Critically

1. Who was Malcolm X? What were his beliefs?
2. Who was Dr. Martin Luther King, Jr.? What were his beliefs?
3. Why were Malcolm X and Dr. Martin Luther King, Jr., important?

Writing

4. Write your own brief biography of a leader from this chapter.
5. Write about an important civil rights organization. Explain why you think it is important today?
6. Imagine that you are Rosa Parks. Write a description or poem telling how you might feel.

AFTER CIVIL RIGHTS, THE STRUGGLE CONTINUES
1970-1990

 In the 1970s, segregation was no longer the law as it was in the 1960s as shown in the photo above. However, African Americans still encountered racism and bias throughout the United States in many areas including education and the job market.

This symbol originated in South Africa and was created to look like a common tsonga pottery motif.

In the 1970s and 1980s, the nation began to put into effect the changes mandated by the Civil Rights Act of 1964. New antidiscrimination laws were passed by Congress. The laws made the nation's racial problems much clearer. Americans were forced to move beyond words and into action. The new laws set new guidelines for behavior in everyday life. It was now time for all citizens to support the democratic ideals stated in the Constitution and the Bill of Rights.

The Vietnam War ended in 1973, and veterans, both black and white, came wearily home. Many were shocked at the conflicts at home. They came home to a still-divided America, an America focused, it seemed, on its own internal conflicts.

 Conflict was not left in Vietnam when the war was over. Many veterans were surprised when they return to a still-divided America.

The Civil Rights Struggle Continues

At the start of the civil rights struggle in the 1950s, President Dwight D. Eisenhower had said, "You cannot legislate the human heart." This proved to be the case with the new antidiscrimination laws. Changes in the workplace and society made many white Americans, both conservative and liberal, protest fiercely. Liberals who had supported African Americans now feared that laws would create quotas and rob them of their jobs. Jobs given to "minority" persons were sometimes seen as jobs no longer available to whites. Most civil rights laws were mainly concerned with employment, housing and education. However, no part of American life was above the new laws. The new legislation made all discrimination unconstitutional.

The issue of busing created some of the greatest conflicts. Busing was an attempt to end segregation in America's public schools. To do this, many public school students were placed on buses and taken to schools in other districts. Many parents, both black and white, argued that the government did not have the right to send children to schools outside their neighborhoods. Some parents did not want African American children brought to the schools in their neighborhood. Schools became battlegrounds.

While many people supported busing, some parents took their children out of public schools and sent them to private schools. Others lobbied their lawmakers to stop busing. Some opponents picketed schools. Others attacked buses with bats and rocks.

To encourage corporations, local governments and schools to act on antidiscrimination laws, the federal government provided special funds, contracts and tax breaks. Affirmative action programs helped students and job applicants of color by setting quotas. The quotas meant that a certain number of jobs were set aside for women and persons of color. In addition, the Equal Employment Opportunity Commission (EEOC) was set up to monitor civil rights in the workplace.

Education and Social Programs

During the 1970s and 1980s, African Americans began to improve their lives with new academic and professional opportunities. The percentage of African Americans graduating from colleges and universities increased. The number of African American professionals (doctors, lawyers, educators, etc.) doubled. More African American-owned businesses were started. The average annual income of African American families also rose. More African American men and women were elected to public office.

During the 1970s, government programs were started to help with social problems such as crime, drugs, unemployment and inadequate housing. Job training centers and programs such as Upward Bound helped train people. Operation Headstart gave meals and early childhood education to the children of low-income families. The Department of Health and Human Services got additional money that could be used to give out more food stamps, as well as additional Medicare and Medicaid health benefits. Government-subsidized, low-income housing was built in urban areas. All these steps helped African Americans and many other people.

The poor were not the only people who benefited from government programs. Social service professionals, as well as teachers and counselors, found their skills in demand. Private construction companies could compete for more contracts to build housing. Jobs for professionals opened up jobs that were now available to everyone by law.

African Americans Continue to Succeed

As African Americans looked for solutions to their problems, they also became more interested in using an important liberty—the right to vote. The right to vote was guaranteed by the Voting Rights Act of 1965. African Americans were elected to the U.S.

House of Representatives. In 1971, these officials united to form the Congressional Black Caucus. African Americans were elected as mayors and representatives in many local governments. Not since the Reconstruction after the Civil War had such a large number of African Americans held public office.

African Americans again suffered some political problems from 1968-1974 because of Republican President Richard Nixon. Nixon tried to slow down or stop desegregation of schools. He cut some funding for some social programs. But Nixon resigned in a scandal in 1974, and Vice-President Gerald Ford finished his term. In 1977, Democrat Jimmy Carter became president and civil rights was once again a priority.

African American pride became the theme, and possibly the most important result, of these turbulent years. Widespread interest in the culture, the history and the accomplishments of African Americans grew. Programs and courses in African American studies appeared in many colleges and universities, as well as in secondary and elementary schools. February was designated as Black History Month. After several years of nationwide lobbying, Dr. King's birthday was declared a national holiday.

Scholars, writers, artists and musicians further incorporated African culture into their creations.

 Unemployment in both urban and rural areas was high during the Depression. It hit African Americans hard. African American workers were the first fired and the last hired.

Setbacks Under Bush and Reagan

Progress rarely remains constant. The nation's economic strength decreased during the 1980s, or Reagan era, and into the Bush years. These Republican years saw increases in military budgets and decreases in budgets for social programs for the poor. The middle class, including African Americans, grew. The number of jobs increased. But the poor had a harder time. The lives of poor Americans especially were hit hard by economic problems. The economy stopped growing and hit a recession.

Interest in the problems of "minorities" took a back seat to the recession. The sacrifices needed to reach economic equality became harder to think about during the recession. Everyone became uneasy about the financial future of themselves and that of the country. The welfare system's support for the poor was seen by many as a drain on the economy. As large corporations cut back, average people worried about their jobs more than their civil rights. The old fears about minority groups taking jobs away from the middle class resurfaced.

 Artists prominent among the leaders of the Committee for the Negro in the Arts included (left to right): Charles White, Janet Collins, Frank Silvera, Viola Scott, Henry A. Wallace

 1. Gerald R. Ford, 38th President (1974-1977)
2. James E. Carter, 39th President (1977-1981)
3. George H.W. Bush, 41st President (1989-1993)

4. Richard M. Nixon, 37th President (1969-1974)
5. Ronald W. Reagan, 40th President (1981-1989)

ACTIVITY

1. Find three examples in Chapter 26 of language that expresses the author's opinion, not just a list of facts. Copy the three examples on a separate sheet of paper and circle the words that told you this was an opinion.

2. Do you agree or disagree with the opinions you identified in #1 above? Write a short essay explaining your own opinion. Support your opinion with facts, as the author did.

3. What did President Eisenhower mean when he said, "You cannot legislate the human heart"? Write an essay, poem, play or other creative expression to describe your explanation. Share it with the class.

CHAPTER 26 REVIEW

Write your answers on a separate piece of paper.

VOCABULARY TO KNOW

Use context clues or a dictionary to help you write definitions for the following words:

1. **antidiscrimination**
2. **minority**
3. **busing**
4. **unconstitutional**
5. **affirmative action**
6. **recession**

Thinking Critically

1. Explain at least three ways the civil rights struggle advanced in the 1970s and 1980s.

2. How did the recession in the 1980s affect civil rights progress in the U.S.?

3. Why was busing started? What do you see as good about busing? What do you see as bad about busing?

Writing

4. Pretend that you are a member of Congress. Write a speech to give to persuade your fellow politicians how to vote on affirmative action.

5. Write a letter to a former president to express your opinion for what kind of job he did. Be fair and base your opinion on fact.

6. Research a civil rights memorial, such as the one in Montgomery, Alabama. Then design your own civil rights memorial. Write a description of it, and include drawings, build a model, or present it in some other form to the class. (Your memorial may also be a drama, dance, or other form of expression.)

WHAT NEXT?
1990-Present

1. **David Dinkins**
   (former Mayor of New York City)
2. **Denzel Washington (actor)**
3. **Toni Morrison (author)**
4. **Colin Powell (Army general,**
   retired as head of the Joint
   Chiefs of Staff)
5. **Jesse Jackson, Jr. &**
   Rev. Jesse Jackson
   (political activists)
6. **Spike Lee (film director)**
7. **Kenneth Chenault (President &**
   COO of American Express)

This symbol originated in the Congo, Kinshasa, and was created to look like Bushongo embroidered cloth design.

George Bush, a Republican, was president for a second term from 1989 to 1993. By the end of his presidency, voters were ready for a change. William Jefferson Clinton became president in 1993 and was reelected in 1996. President Clinton, a Democrat, dominates the 1990s.

However, Clinton has not been a Democrat in the liberal tradition. He has not supported social programs for the poor as Democrats did in the past. The Democratic Party and President Clinton are more conservative than in the past. Perhaps one reason for this is that Congress has been controlled by Republicans in the 1990s. The President has to compromise to get congressional approval for his programs.

Former Head of the Joint Chiefs of Staff, Colin Powell

In Clinton's first term, the economic recession of the Bush years ended. Perhaps, with a healthy economy and a growing African American middle class, more people are becoming conservative, less willing to push for changes. Or perhaps the changes are less newsworthy than in past decades.

African Americans continue to make progress in elections to important government positions. By 1997, there was one African American senator, Carol Mosley Braun. There were thirty-seven African American members of the House of Representatives, twenty-seven men and ten women. African American mayors numbered 417. There were African American governors of states.

Senator Carol Mosley Braun

Politically, African Americans voted more. Colin Powell, an Army general, retired as head of the Joint Chiefs of Staff in 1993. With each presidential election, many people hope he will run and become the first African American President. We will have to wait until the next decade to see if he changes his mind and runs for President.

The Supreme Court remains conservative, reflecting the appointments to it by Presidents Reagan and Bush. The great civil rights lawyer and supreme court justice Thurgood Marshall retired in 1991. An African American, Clarence Thomas, was appointed in his place. Justice Thomas is conservative, however.

Politically, no single African American leader has emerged in the 1990s as a strong leader like Malcolm X or Dr. Martin Luther King, Jr. Instead, a number of philosophies exist. Afrocentric scholars argue for the need for an African-centered view, with African Americans keeping their own cultural links. Conservatives such as Ward Connerly, an adviser to President Clinton, argue that African Americans do not need any special viewpoint or help, as they can make it on their own now without help from government. Scholars such as Henry Louis Gates, Jr., present an intellectual view of African American achievement, mostly staying out of the political world and in the academic world. Louis Farrakhan, head of the Nation of Islam, was outspoken in calling on black Muslims to follow Islam. He also had meetings for African American men, calling on them to be responsible family heads.

A growing African American middle class seems to feel that less change is needed now. Opinion polls say different things. When Ward Connerly took a poll, he found that most people, both African American and white, support prohibiting the governement from giving special treatment to anyone. When other groups take polls, the opposite results are sometimes found. One thing is sure—gone are the days of the Civil Rights Movement. A new conservativism is popular. Issues that African Americans fought for in the past are now being reexamined. Affirmative Action, busing, and even desegregation are no longer seen by the middle class as needed changes.

Thurgood Marshall

 Louis Farrakhan, leader of the Nation of Islam, speaking at the
Million Man March on October 16, 1995 in Washington, D.C.

Instead, these programs are being examined for good and bad. For example, some African American people now see busing as harmful because neighborhoods were broken up and more African American children had to ride buses than white children.

African American men in the 1990s reacted to the way many saw them, and organized to do better. Many African Americans saw African American men as not taking enough responsibility for their families, children, and themselves. The Million Man March in 1995 was a march of African American men in Washington, D.C. The march served to band them together with support for each other. It also was a public way to say, "We take responsibility." Other movements and groups continued this trend throughout the country.

IN OUR OWN IMAGE

African Americans Embrace Socially through Arts, Culture, Education and Economic Empowerment

With the growth of an African American middle class with more money to spend, the number of African American and African products grew, too. Fashions, magazines, toys and other industries made popular products that were distinctly African American. Businesses grew up around these products.

In the arts, African Americans have entered a second renaissance period. Actors such as Denzel Washington and Whoopi Goldberg are being joined by an increasing number of successful African American actors, both in movies and on TV. Directors such as Spike Lee and John Singleton are being joined by others in directing new films. In music, African Americans continue to lead the way with new musical styles, such as rap and hip-hop. Queen Latifah led the way in rap. And music producers such as Sean "Puffy" Combs are new powers in the industry. Hip-hop artist Chris Parker, known as KRS-1, is seen by many as a philosopher as well as a musical artist.

The world of art, sculpture, and dance have exploded with African American artists. Many include African influences in their creations. In the literary world, African Americans broke another barrier in 1993 when Toni Morrison became the first African American woman to win the Nobel Prize in Literature. Toni Morrison is one of many African American writers who is leaving her mark as a literary great, coming to recognition in the 1990s.

In education, African Americans still work for change. Many colleges have programs in African American history. Some even offer graduate degrees. Many public high schools now offer African American history courses, but not all. But few elementary or middle school/junior high schools offer such courses. In 1993, the Detroit Public Schools made history by passing a resolution to make the curriculum Afrocentric. But so far, they are the only public school district to take such a step for their whole district. Multicultural curriculums are common. But "multicultural" means very little change from the 1970s in some districts, and means including a little information about many cultures in other districts. Overall, history in the public schools is still heavily European American.

The split between the African American middle class and the African American poor widened in the 1990s, too.

Much progress continues to be made, but the 1990s have been a conservative decade of self-examination. The amount of real, lasting change remains to be seen, but there is no doubt that African Americans will continue to be influential in most areas of American life.

1. Maya Angelou (author)
2. Angella Bassett (actress)
3. Cuba Gooding, Jr. (actor)
4. Janet Jackson (singer/actress)
5. Quincy Jones
   (musician & producer)

6. Luther Vandross
   (singer & musician)
7. Alice Walker (author)
8. Oprah Winfrey (talk show host)
9. Will Smith (actor)
10. Michael Johnson (athlete)
11. En Vogue (musical group)

12. Prince (singer & musician)
13. Whitney Houston
    (singer/actress)
14. Sinbad (comedian/actor)
15. Tiger Woods (athlete)
16. Tyson Beckford (model)

IN OUR OWN IMAGE

ACTIVITY

1. Make a poster of African American artists who, in your opinion, are part of the second renaissance. Include their names, a description of what their artistic field is, and an explanation of why you think they are important.

2. Create your own expression of African American achievement. Your expression may take any form—dance, rap, song, poetry, etc. Write a short explanation of your expression and share it with the class. Then perform your expression.

3. What do you think of President Clinton's accomplishments? Has he been a good president for African Americans? Write a speech explaining your thoughts. Support your opinions with facts. Give your speech for the class.

CHAPTER 27 REVIEW

Write your answers on a separate piece of paper.

VOCABULARY TO KNOW

Use context clues or a dictionary to help you write definitions for the following words:

1. conservative
2. liberal
3. middle class
4. trend
5. curriculum
6. multicultural

Thinking Critically

1. Describe at least three important changes in the 1990s for African Americans. Tell why you see each as important.

2. How might a conservative President and a conservative supreme court slow down the progress of African Americans?

3. Do you think an African American president of the U.S. would be different from white presidents? Why?

Writing

4. Choose a current African American leader. Create a poster with explanations of why his or her contributions are important.

5. Choose an African American artist in any field in which you are interested. Research his or her creations. Write a report about his or her work. Present it to the class.

6. Choose an African American writer and read at least one story or book of his or her. Write a book report on it. Present your report to the class. Explain why you think the writer is good or bad. Explain whether or not you think the writer is important for African American students to read, and tell why.

VOCABULARY WORDS

abolish
abolitionist
absorb
abuse
agreement
ally
almanac
amendment
Ancestor
apathy
artisan
astronomy
attitude
blacksmith
bond
bondage
Cabinet
catnapped
civilization
class
complex
compromise
compromise
compromise
concession
conclusion
contribution
convention
creditor
creed
crisis
cultivate
culture
deed
degrade
dehydration
democracy
democracy
deprive

descendant
discrimination
dispute
document
emotion
encourage
enforce
engineering
equality
expedition
familiar
forbade
framer
geographic
harvested
hemisphere
hypocrisy
immigrant
indenture
insurrection
integrate
invention
issue
justice
liberty
limits
literacy exploit
lynch
mason
mason
media
merchant
mission
mutilate
mutiny
noble
oppose
oppress
origin

overseer
pardon
petition
plantation
plentiful
political party
politics
prejudice
principle
prod
professional
protest
protest
quota
rebellion
Reconstruction
recruit
refuge
resistance
respect
revolt
revolt
salvation
segregation
segregation
self-reliance
sharecropping
skirmish
society
status
subdue
suffocation
superior
survey
tactic
terrorist
value
visible

INDEX

INDEX

INDEX

INDEX

INDEX

top right	Harriett Tubman (c. 1821-1913), known for her courage in guiding enslaved people to freedom on the "underground railroad"
middle right	Rosa Parks, who refused to sit in the back of the bus in the "colored section" and was arrested for this action in December, 1955, starting a legal challenge to segregation that went to the Supreme Court a year later, and resulted in segregation being ruled unconstitutional.
middle right, left of Rosa Parks	Martin Delaney was an abolitionist and the highest rankingAfrican American officer in the Union Army during the Civil War.
bottom right	Part of the Harlem Renaissance, Marcus Garvey founded the Universal Negro Improvement Association in 1914, and was the leader of a movement for African American pride.
middle bottom, left of Marcus Garvey	Toni Morrison became the first African American woman to win the Nobel Prize for Literature in 1993 after winning the Pulitzer Prize for Literature earlier.
bottom left	Thurgood Marshall was the first African American Justice on the Supreme Court, serving from 1967 to 1991. His earlier legal successes as a lawyer for civil rights cases are landmark decisions, the most famous being Brown v. Board of Education of Topeka, Kansas, which he won before the Supreme Court in 1954, ending school segregation.
middle left	Reverend Doctor Martin Luther King, Jr. (1929-1978, assassinated), perhaps the most noted leader of the Civil Rights movement who worked peacefully to end discrimination and poverty
middle, right of Dr. King	Sojourner Truth was born enslaved in 1797 in the state of New York and freed by New York state law in 1827. A famous abolitionist, she traveled working to end slavery and as a speaker convinced many to work with her. She also worked for women's rights.
middle, center	Malcolm X (1925-1965, assassinated) became a leader of the Nation of Islam in the United States and was a powerful philosophical Civil Rights leader for many, expressing his beliefs in the rights of African Americans to full equality.
top left, above Dr. King	photo from the Million Man March on Washington, D.C., in 1995, in which African American men united to express their commitment to responsibility as African American men to grow a strong African American community
top left	photo of an African landscape with an African elephant roaming free
headband on woman	diagram of a middle passage slave ship showing how enslaved African people were packed in
African woman	The woman is an artist's painting and represents Mother Africa.

PHOTO CREDITS

Cover Credits

top row, l to r, National Geographic, National Archives; middle row, l to r, Archive Photo, Northwind Picture Archives, Sketch by Steve Covallo, National Archives, Northwind Picture Archives, PPG Archives; bottom row, l to r, PPG Archives, Library Of Congress

Interior Credits

p. 2, Northwind Picture Archives; p. 3, PPG Archives; p. 5, Northwind Picture Archives; p. 6, Black Studies Resources, The William Loren Katz Collection; p. 7, Northwind Picture Archives; p. 8, Black Studies Resources, The William Loren Katz Collection; p. 10, Northwind Picture Archives; pp. 12, 13, (left) Archive Photo, (right) Black Studies Resources, The William Loren Katz Collection; p. 14, (left) Black Studies Resources, The William Loren Katz Collection; p. 15, Northwind Picture Archives; p. 16, Black Studies Resources, The William Loren Katz Collection; p. 18, Northwind Picture Archives; p. 19, sketch by Armando Baez; p. 20, Northwind Picture Archives; p. 21, PPG Archives; p. 22 & 23, Black Studies Resources, The William Loren Katz Collection; p 24, Northwind Picture Archives; p. 26, Black Studies Resources, The William Loren Katz Collection; pp. 28, 30, Northwind Picture Archives; pp. 31,32 & 34, Northwind Picture Archives; p. 35, Library of Congress; pp. 36 & 37, Black Studies Resources, The William Loren Katz Collection; pp. 38, 40-41, Northwind Picture Archives; p. 42, National Archives; pp. 43-44, National Archives; p. 45, Black Studies Resources, The William Loren Katz Collection; p. 46, PPG Archives; p. 48, Northwind Picture Archives; p. 49, Archive Photo; p. 51, Black Studies Resources, The William Loren Katz Collection, p. 52, PPG Archives; p. 56, Northwind Picture Archives; p. 57, (left) Black Studies Resources, The William Loren Katz Collection, (right) PPG Archives; p. 58, Library of Congress; p. 59, PPG Archives; p. 60, Black Studies Resources, The William Loren Katz Collection; pp. 61, Northwind Picture Archives; p. 62, Black Studies Resources, The William Loren Katz Collection; p. 64, Northwind Picture Archives; p. 65-66, Black Studies Resources, The William Loren Katz Collection; pp. 67- 68, Archive Photo; p. 69, sketch by Armando Baez; p. 70, Library of Congress and Northwind Picture Archives; p. 71, Archive Photo; p. 72,74, Black Studies Resources, The William Loren Katz Collection; p. 76, Northwind Picture Archives; p. 77, Black Studies Resources, The William Loren Katz Collection; p. 78, (left, top and bottom) Black Studies Resources, The William Loren Katz Collection, (right) National Archives; p. 79, Library of Congress; p. 80, Black Studies Resources, The William Loren Katz Collection and Library of Congress; p. 83 & 84, Black Studies Resources, The William Loren Katz Collection; p. 85, Black Studies Resources, The William Loren Katz Collection; p. 86, PPG Archives; p. 88, Library of Congress; p. 90, National Archives; p. 91, PPG Archives; p. 94, Black Studies Resources, The William Loren Katz Collection, sketches by Armando Baez; p. 95, Black Studies Resources, The William Loren Katz Collection; p. 96, Library of Congress; pp. 97-98, Black Studies Resources, The William Loren Katz Collection; p. 102, Black Studies Resources, The William Loren Katz Collection; p. 104, Northwind Picture Archives; p. 105, Black Studies Resources, The William Loren Katz Collection; p. 106, Northwind Picture Archives; p. 107, Black Studies Resources, The William Loren Katz Collection; p. 109, Library of Congress; p. 110, PPG Archives; p. 112, National Archives; p. 116, Library of Congress; p. 117, Northwind Picture Archives; p. 118, Northwind Picture Archives; p. 119, Northwind Picture Archives; p. 122, Black Studies Resources, The William Loren Katz Collection; p. 124, Library of Congress; p. 125-126, Library of Congress; p. 127, Black Studies Resources, The William Loren Katz Collection; p. 128, PPG Archives; p. 130, Library of Congress; p. 131, Black Studies Resources, The William Loren Katz Collection; p. 133 134, 136, The Schomburg Center for Research in Black Culture; p. 137, National Archives; p. 138, Library of Congress; p. 139, Black Studies Resources, The William Loren Katz Collection; pp. 140-141, Library of Congress; p. 142, Black Studies Resources, The William Loren Katz Collection; pp. 144-146, Black Studies Resources, The William Loren Katz Collection; p. 147, Northwind Picture Archives; 148,150, Black Studies Resources, The William Loren Katz Collection; p. 151, Archive Photo; pp. 152-154, Black Studies Resources, The William Loren Katz Collection; pp. 156, 157, National Archives; Black Studies Resources, The William Loren Katz Collection; pp. 158-159, National Archives; p. 162, PPG Archives; Archive Photo, Black Studies Resources, The William Loren Katz Collection, "Lift Every Voice and Sing", copyright 1917, 1921, 1935 by James Weldon Johnson, copyright renewed (c) 1963 by Grace Nail Johnson, from Saint Peter Relates An Incident by James Weldon Johnson. Used by permission of Viking Penguin, a division of Penguin books USA Inc.; p. 164, AP Wideworld Photo; p. 165, National Archives; pp. 167,170, Black Studies Resources, The William Loren Katz Collection; p. 171, National Archives; p. 172, PPG Archives and Black Studies Resources, The William Loren Katz Collection; p. 173, National Archives; p. 174, Black Studies Resources, The William Loren Katz Collection; p. 176, PPG Archives; p. 178, The Final Call Newspaper and PPG Archives; p. 179, PPG Archives; p. 180-181, Lyndon B. Johnson Presidential Library; pp. 182,184, PPG Archives; p. 185, Archive Photo; p. 187-188, PPG Archives; p. 189, PPG Archives; p. 190, Eisenhower Presidential Library; p. 192, Archive Photo, Library of Congress; p. 193, Archive Photo; p. 194, PPG Archives; p. 195, 197 & 198, Archive Photo; special thanks to Robert Siller for providing definitions for African symbols

NOTES

NOTES

NOTES